If ever there was someone qualified by life experience to author a book about crystals it would be Rachelle Charman. For Rachelle, each crystal has a consciousness, a spirit, a life force that emanates a vibration of ancient wisdom; a wisdom potent enough to help us remember so much about who and what we are and why we're here. Rachelle is not the first person to espouse such a connection to the mineral kingdom, but while I deeply respect the connection other authors may have, for me personally, no one champions their deep magick as tangibly and as believably as Rachelle Charman.

Scott Alexander King, www.animaldreaming.com

Rachelle's passion for healing and the mineral kingdom shine through her beautiful meditations and gemstone communications. She has written a well rounded guide to help anyone begin on their gemstone journey.

Naisha Ahsian - The Book of Stones

When I first met Rachelle I knew I was in the presence of a very special spiritual person. Her energy is pure and her honesty and sincerity shine through like a beacon which attracts people to her. It is her nature to help others and her destiny to display her gifts in this world. Rachelle has many great abilities and spiritual virtues that she shares with her students on the spiritual path.

Gordon Smith, author and the UK's most accurate medium

Rachelle's love and knowledge of the crystals is inspiring. Learning from her is a healing, empowering experience.

Lucy Cavendish, witch and author

✦ ✦ ✦

CRYSTALS

Understand and connect to the
medicine and healing of crystals

RACHELLE CHARMAN

ROCKPOOL
PUBLISHING

A Rockpool book
PO Box 252
Summer Hill
NSW 2130
Australia
www.rockpoolpublishing.com.au
http://www.facebook.com/RockpoolPublishing

First published in 2012
Copyright © Rachelle Charman, 2012

National Library of Australia Cataloguing-in-Publication entry
Charman, Rachelle.

Crystals: understand and connect to the medicine and healing power of crystals / Rachelle Charman.

9781921878701 (pbk.)

Includes index.

Crystals--Therapeutic use.
Precious stones--Therapeutic use.
133.2548

Edited by Catherine Spedding Editorial Services
Cover design by Seymour Design
Internal design by Ingrid Kwong
Illustrations by Lisa Shillan

Images: Tiger's Eye: **Weinrich Minerals, Inc, www.weinrichmineralsinc.com**; Spirit quartz: **www.heartoftheearth.com.au**; Ajoite, Amazonite, Apatite — Green, Aquamarine, Aragonite, Azurite, Bixbite, Brazilianite, Bustamite, Calcite, Chrysocolla, Danburite, Diamond, Diopside, Dioptase, Emerald, Kunzite, Morganite, Phenacite, Purpurite, Pyrite, Tanzanite, Topaz, Tourmaline — Blue, Green, Pink and Red: **Rob Lavinsky, www.mineralatlas.com**; Black Obsidian, Aventurine, Agate, Amber, Amethyst, Ametrine, Andalusite — Chiastolite, Angelite, Apache Tears, Apophyllite, Barnacle, Tourmaline — Black and Brown, Bloodstone, Boji Stones™, Blue Lace Agate, Cacoxenite, Cathedral Lightbrary, Celestite, Channelling Dow, Chrysoprase, Citrine, Crocoite, Devic Temple, Double Terminator, Dumortierite, Elestial, Eudialyte, Fluorite, Fulgurite, Galena, Golden Calcite, Grounding Crystal, Helidor, Herkimer, Hiddenite, Isis, Jade, Jasper — Mookite, Ocean and Red, Jet, Key, Labradorite, Lapis Lazuli, Larimar, Laser Wand, Lemurian Seeded, Libyan Gold Tektite, Manifestation Crystal, Moldavite, Moonstone, Nirvana Quartz, Nuummite, Orpiment, Pietersite, Phantom, Prehnite, Pyromorphite, Quartz, Rainbow Crystal, Record Keeper, Rhodonite, Rose Quartz, Ruby, Scolecite, Selenite, Self Healed, Seraphinite, Serpentine, Shaman Stone, Shattuckite, Shiva Lingam, Sodalite, Smoky Quartz, Spirit Quartz, Sungite, Sunstone, Surgilite, Tabby, Tantric Twin, Tektite, Tibetan Quartz, Tiger Eye, Time Link, Transmitter, Turquoise, Vivianite, Window, Zincite, Fairy Stone, Tree Root, Malachite and Azurite, Malachite and Chrysocolla: **Matt Walker, www. facebook.com/MattWalkerImages**; Apatite — Blue, Carnelian, Charoite, Chrysanthemum Stone, Chrysoberyl, Cinnabar, Crocoite, Cuprite, Fire Agate, Garnet, Goethite, Hematite, Kyanite — Blue, Lepidolite, Malachite, Natrolite, Opal, Peridot, Petrified Wood, Rodochrosite, Rutilated Quartz, Stibnite, Watermelon Tourmaline: **John H. Betts, www. johnbetts-fineminerals.com**

Thank you to The Wizard of Auz for the use of some images supplied with Matt Walker. The Wizard of Auz sources and trades globally. They are especially known for their extensive range of rare and unusual crystals and gemstones, which they supply as natural forms, carvings and shapes, or beads and trinkets. They are members of the Fair Trade Association of Australia and New Zealand and are very conscientious about product sourcing and ethics; **www.wizardofauz.com, www.facebook.com/wizauz,** Twitter @WizardofAuz. In Australia 1-800 THE WIZARD.

Printed in China

10 9 8 7 6

About Rachelle

Rachelle Charman is the founder and principal of The Academy of Crystal Awakening. She spends her free time in union and ceremony with sacred land, honouring Mother Earth and sharing in her ancient wisdom. Rachelle receives her teachings directly from her own life experiences, the Crystal Kingdom and Mother Earth herself as she truly embodies and radiates her deep wisdom. In her powerful connection to the Crystal Kingdom and understanding of the healing gifts and tools of the Earth, Rachelle has received profound healing and experienced a deep awakening of the self.

Rachelle's teachings are truly dynamic, heartfelt and life changing. In her deep passion for assisting humanity in embracing self-love and acceptance, Rachelle offers her fellow students her advanced knowledge in the healing gifts offered by the Crystal Kingdom, those special gems and stones that can only be considered as a gift from Heaven to Earth.

By taking a step into your heart and learning the healing powers and processes offered by Rachelle, the Crystal Kingdom and Mother Earth, you will open up to a world of self-healing where unconditional love fills every cell of your being. Crystals embody not only simplistic beauty, but a multitude of energies that activate our mind, body and soul. Rachelle certainly embodies their gifts and knowledge.

Rachelle's teachings flow naturally from the heart and are strongly driven by her love of humanity. She embodies and lives her divine mission for sharing her love of and passion for the Earth's medicines. She is recognised globally for her depth and authenticity. Rachelle is a dynamic and passionate teacher, and travels the world with her teachings, paving the way for others to reconnect to their own innate shamanic wisdom and realign to the organic flow of Mother Earth's love, healing and wisdom. She is well known throughout the world for her organic, loving, down-to-earth personality and truly radiates Divine Love.

Rachelle has spent time with Peruvian shamans and native healers in the Amazon, where she witnessed and experienced profound healings and gained much insight into the healing ways of the native tribes. While in Peru, her own memory and deep-held knowledge of shamanic healing was activated. She is a natural healer and teacher who lives life guided by the flow of her divinely loving heart.

Rachelle worked for Hay House Australia for three years. She was Doreen Virtue's Australian assistant and head of the Angel Intuitive mentor group, where she supported almost 2000 certified Angel Initiatives. She worked beside some of the world's most renowned spiritual leaders, including Louise Hay, Gordon Smith, Dr Wayne W Dyer, Sonia Choquette, Deepak Chopra, John Edward, John Holland, Eric Pearl and many more. Rachelle contributed a crystal healing chart to Doreen Virtue's *Angel Medicine*.

Rachelle has been inspired by many amazing teachers on her journey of self-discovery. She has been deeply inspired by her crystal healing teacher, Maggie Vrinda Ross, who assisted her in awakening to the knowledge of the Crystal Kingdom. Rachelle's teachings are aligned to Maggie and Katrina Raphaell, Maggie's teacher. Rachelle has experienced deep transformation and healing working with these teachings, and from her profound awakenings and experiences has developed her own style and wisdom.

RACHELLE CHARMAN
Founder of *The Academy of Crystal Awakening*
www.crystalawakening.com
info@crystalawakening.com

Acknowledgements

It's been such an amazing journey and I would not be the person I am today without the loving support and guidance of all the beautiful people I have met along the way. This book has certainly been nurtured and birthed with the support and existence of these wonderful souls. Please allow me to share my deep gratitude and love.

I would first like to share a huge, heartfelt thank you to the loving beings of the Crystal Kingdom. Thank you for sharing your love and wisdom with me and coming into my life at exactly the right time to shine your light into my soul. Thank you for the deep, profound healing I have experienced and received. I would not be the person I am today without your guidance and ongoing support. I am truly honoured to be a voice for your loving community and am deeply blessed to know and feel you in my life. Thank you to all my loving guides and Angels in spirit for your patience and gentle persistence from the other side. Thank you to my powerful spirit animals for your continuous healing and guidance in my life.

I would like to share my deep honour and love for our amazing planet, Mother Gaia. You have held, nurtured and guided me with every step and breath I have taken here on Earth. We are one and I feel your loving vibration and heartbeat resonate deep into mine. Thank you for sharing your ancient wisdom with me and guiding me home to my heart.

To all the beautiful teachers in the physical world I have met on my journey, you have all shared your heart and deep wisdom with me, allowing me to shine in all my essence. I would also like to share my deep gratitude to Maggie Vrinda Ross, my amazing crystal healing teacher. Thank you for seeing my light, and loving and nurturing me when I could not love myself. I would not be the person I am today without you. Thank you Doreen Virtue for introducing me to the Angelic Realm, and supporting me to step into my power and to believe in myself. You truly are a shining light in my life and many other souls here on Earth. Thank you to Leon Nacson for allowing such an amazing opportunity to turn myself around and make something of my life. To my powerful shaman in Peru, Edwin, thank you for igniting the deep fire within of my own shamanic wisdom.

I would not be able to share the love and wisdom of the Crystal Kingdom if it was not for the support and love of all the students and teachers of The Academy of Crystal Awakening. I love you all and thank you for allowing me to shine my light on the world.

Thank you to all the beautiful friends and soul family I have met on my journey. I hold and share a piece of your heart in mine; thank you for loving me. A special thank you to Alex for gifting me my first crystal, and to Jo for planting and watering the seeds for this book. Love you sweet sisters. Thank you to Tania for taking me in off the street all those years ago and seeing my heart and true essence.

Thank you to Lisa and all the crew at Rockpool Publishing for seeing and believing in my vision, and feeling my passion for this book. Thanks to Scott Alexander King for your love and support in the birthing of Crystals.

Thanks to Matt for all the hours you put in to capture some of the most amazing photos of crystals I have ever seen. Thank you for bringing out the magic and essence of the crystals so they can shine their light on many. Thank you to the beautiful Wendy and Sean from Wizard of Auz in Byron Bay for opening up your hearts and sacred space to me, and allowing us to shoot some of your powerful crystals for this book.

A big thank you to my family for loving me unconditionally so I could follow my dreams and be the best I can be in life.

To my beautiful dog, Gaia, thank you for teaching me unconditional love at its purest.

To my beautiful, beloved Yvette, thank you for shining your loving light into my heart and walking beside me as we share this journey together. You make my life and heart complete.

Rachelle Charman

Contents

PART 1

Understanding the Crystal Kingdom
and their ancient healing wisdom

Introduction

This book is a gift to you, the reader, from my heart to assist you on your deep journey of transformation and awakening as you connect to and explore the Crystal Kingdom and its magic. The information in this book will guide and encourage you to have your own experiences with the Crystal Kingdom as you bring through your own wisdom and knowledge of this powerful medicine from the Earth.

The intention for this book is for you to empower yourself on your journey through life. All of us are searching in some way for a tool that can assist us in moving through our challenges into a place of empowerment and joy in our lives. We sometimes search outside ourselves looking for the answers. I truly believe everything we need to know lies within each and every one of us, now and always. The beauty of crystals is they inspire us to delve deep within ourselves as we connect to our own internal wisdom and knowledge. Please take what feels right within the pages of this book and leave what doesn't and, more importantly, find your own way and your own connection to your heart and divine mission here on Earth. This workbook is like a blank canvas that is offered to you to create and paint your own picture, assisting you in finding your own way — your own deep wisdom — and empowering the healer that lies within as you embark on your magical journey with the Crystal Kingdom.

This book is created as a step-by-step guide with simple yet powerful processes and exercises on how to cleanse, charge, program and connect to crystals, encouraging you to have a tangible experience of your own, promoting deep self-transformation and personal empowerment. Also included are ways to create crystal essences, working with the Teacher Crystals (Master Crystals), crystals and the chakras, and simple healing techniques and meditations.

The second section of the book lists various crystals and the meanings of their medicine. Underneath each crystal is a blank section for you to write your own experience of its energy. Throughout this book you will be offered several processes, assisting you to create a deep connection between you and the crystal supporting and enhancing your own experience. Once you integrate each individual crystal and its energy, ensure you record the healing that occurred in your life and within yourself at that time. This healing will mirror and relate directly to the healing vibration of the specific crystal. As you embark on this journey it will guide you to a deeper level of self-healing and awakening of self as you start to facilitate your own connection and healing with the crystals, creating your own unique crystal reference book.

In the third section of the book you are invited into the world of other people's experiences and interactions. These experiences include several powerful and life-changing stories and case studies on how crystals have assisted and facilitated healing and transformation on the physical, emotional, mental and spiritual levels. It is always inspiring to hear other people's experiences as they open, deepen and ground your own experience and understanding. Many of the stories have been offered and shared by the teachers and students of The Academy of Crystal Awakening.

This is an active workbook so at times you will be required to work with the physical crystal. You can purchase many of the crystals from your local new age shops and gem shops. The Academy of Crystal Awakening also has for sale on our website crystals that are specially infused and charged with Divine Love energy. I personally invoke the Devas with the intention of healing using the processes in this book.

As you read through and experience each chapter you will be guided and supported to journey deep within the Crystal Kingdom and its medicine of love. On this journey you will unlock and bring forth your own wisdom and knowledge, awakening to your own divine truth. Creating your own unique connection with the Crystal Kingdom is an essential and, I believe, very important part of your own healing process. Owning and listening to your own inner wisdom is important for truly stepping into your power.

Over the years I have had my own life-changing experiences with the healing power of the Crystal Kingdom, and it is my passion and vision to offer this opportunity to those who are also drawn to these amazing gifts. Crystals have assisted in creating many miracles in my life, allowing me to shine in my totality. Crystals are singing more than ever on our planet at this time and are calling people from all walks of life. The information offered in Crystals has already assisted thousands of people through my workshops on their healing journey, creating self-love, wellbeing and inner peace. Many people have found a new depth of belief in themselves and discovered renewed inspiration and purpose. I feel truly blessed to assist in bringing hope and inspiration to you and a tool to assist you to create more wellbeing and inner peace in your life.

We can invite crystals into our lives in various different ways. Having these beautiful crystals in the home creates an environment for transformation. You can sit quietly with your crystal, simply setting your intention to tune into its healing energy. You will also benefit from a crystal's healing properties simply by holding, wearing, or having a crystal in your pocket because your energy field will start to mirror the energy field of the crystal's pure structure, bringing balance and healing.

I truly believe crystals are gifts from Mother Earth, to support us on our divine journey back to love. As we connect and work with crystals we create divine union with and reconnection to our Mother Earth and our source, experiencing oneness and joy.

Please know and remember my heart is with you as you embark on this sacred journey into the Crystal Kingdom.

CRYSTAL AWAKENING –
MY PERSONAL JOURNEY

For thousands of years the ancients have been pointing to this time in history on Earth. It is recorded in the ancient texts and calendars that this is a time of powerful awakening and transformation. They called the time in which we are living the New Age. This is a time of new awareness as we journey deeper into our hearts with the understanding that we are all of one essence, the essence of love. We are being called to seed a new consciousness into the planet, one that comes from a place deep within our hearts as we start to create a world of love and oneness, connecting back to our tribes, creating harmony and wellbeing in our lives.

The veil of the worlds is lifting as we journey towards the cosmic kiss, the marring of the dimensions. We are transcending from a third and fourth dimensional reality to a fifth dimensional reality where we hold more love and peace within our hearts. The magnetic fields of Earth are becoming less powerful as we become more light sensitive, and more aware spiritually, emotionally, mentally and physically. As our Mother Earth lessens in magnetic energy and quickens in vibration we have all been given the opportunity to heal and become more aware, to release the old belief systems and emotions that no longer serve us in this lifetime.

I believe that crystals have an important role to play in this transformation, as more and more souls awaken and truly start to understand the powerful healing qualities of crystals, and the divinity and power within our own hearts. Crystals amplify and bring more light into our being, enabling and supporting us in healing and transformation as they bring us back into our pure natural state of being. We are all loving, all knowing and all wise as we remember our oneness and connection with All That Is. Our seeds of love and hope, that have been planted and nurtured over the years, have finally sprouted and we are manifesting our dreams and ambitions. This is the time of the awakening of the heart and we are so privileged to be here on Earth at such an exciting time. Our heart opens as we experience compassion and an awareness of how precious and beautiful we are, sparking within a calling for us to nurture and love ourselves, those around us, and the Earth. In this connection a deep healing and awakening of self is created and shared in this sacred journey called life.

Crystals have been a major part of my awakening and healing on this journey of self-discovery and I would like to share with you my experience of this transformation as we all venture into this time of the New Age. We all have our story, our past, our experiences that makes us who we are today. I spent most of the first 28 years of my life walking asleep. I felt like I was running from a deep pain that lay dormant within me. I found myself running away from home, living on the streets and running from myself to numb the pain. I felt a deep sadness, depression and anxiety in my life. Over the years of healing I have come to understand and realise that these powerful life lessons and experiences have made me who I am today, and I have come to a place of gratitude and peace in my heart for choosing this powerful path of growth.

Around 2000 I started becoming aware of a new feeling within, which brought with it a new understanding that there was more to life than simply just existing. I was gifted a powerful Amethyst Crystal by a dear friend. I had no idea what crystals were at that time, what energy was; I did not even know who I was. One night I was holding the crystal in one hand and my whole physical body started to vibrate. I found myself in a place of pure bliss. This experience lasted for days as I saw things in my past that I had been a victim to. I was able to see these things in a new light, able to see the lessons and gifts that came with such challenge. With this expanded awareness and awakening came much healing and nurturing to my soul.

A deep spiritual awakening had occurred and it brought light to the darkest parts of my being. A spark of deep passion was ignited within to learn more about the Crystal Kingdom and what it had to offer. I completed three intense crystal healing workshops with a beautiful lady, my teacher Maggie Vrinda Ross. Everything we learnt, I experienced — it was like a flower blossoming within as I started to remember the sacred healing power of crystals. I believe if you are attracted to crystals you have known them before, so it becomes a process of remembering and reawakening this sacred knowledge within.

I then found myself working for Hay House Australia as Doreen Virtue's assistant, as well as travelling and working with many amazing spiritual teachers. After learning much about the Angelic Realm, where I witnessed and experienced many miracles, I was called to travel to South America where I spent time working with a Peruvian shaman by the name of Edwin. Once again I was given the opportunity to awaken my inner knowing and knowledge of the healing ways of the shaman.

I now live in my homeland of Australia and have created and birthed The Academy of Crystal Awakening, with more than 3000 students and 26 teachers in Australia, New Zealand and China. I travel and teach the magical powers of crystals and truly love what I do. I am blessed to share my passion for and love of healing. I deeply believe if we do what we love in life and follow our hearts, manifestation is organic. I also know that if I am now travelling the world teaching about crystal healing, walking my path, that every single one of you can do what you love and what you are here to do too. The secret is to open and follow your heart with strength, courage and unconditional love for yourself, your tribe and our Divine Mother Earth.

I have come to understand that healing is not about fixing anything, rather it's an experience of expanded awareness, acceptance and surrender as we realise that we are divine beings of light on this journey of love. Experiencing ourselves in all forms, from the light to the dark, we shall know ourselves in all ways as an expression of Divine Love.

CRYSTALS

Crystals are divine gifts and sacred tools from Mother Earth that assist us in our growth, transformation and healing. They are one of the many medicines of the planet, with each crystal holding a specific energy that can assist us in our healing process. The Earth is made up of 85 per cent crystal, so in reality we are living on one big ball of crystal.

Crystals are definitely more than just pretty rocks, they're alive and have a consciousness of their own. I believe that all crystals hold unique, loving energies that assist humanity in discovering our true divine magnificence. As we connect to a crystal and its energy, it allows us to align and connect to the same healing energy that exists within each of us. Crystals radiate Divine Love and pure energy from Mother Earth and the universe, and amplify and reflect back to us the beauty within our hearts, allowing us the opportunity to heal ourselves. In this process, our emotional, mental, spiritual and physical bodies can attain balance. Crystals encourage and assist us to live in the now so we start to truly understand that we are all connected to the universe at all times. Crystals remind us of our true essence of oneness and connection to source.

So you can get a deeper understanding of how this works, I would like to share with you a little information about the science of crystals and our sacred connection to them. Everything in this universe is made up of energy and vibration. The science that explains this is Sacred Geometry, which is an in-depth study of how everything in the universe is connected to the one source — universal energy. There are five main shapes, or blueprints, that energy organises and aligns itself to as it manifests into the physical form. All life on the planet stems from these shapes, called the five platonic solids.

Crystals are pure energy made up of atoms. These atoms are the inner structure of energy. Crystals are formed and birthed when these atoms of energy align to different forms, the platonic solids. This process allows each crystal to be unique, each holding a different energy, colour and vibration. Everything on this physical plane is created from these energetic structures, all vibrating at different frequencies with different combinations of these atoms aligning through the five platonic solids and Sacred Geometry. This tells us that everything is connected to the same universal source at our core.

The sacred relationship that's created between us and the Crystal Kingdom allows for deep transformation and healing to occur on many levels. Crystals hold within them the secrets to healing as they assist humanity in our journey back to peace and wellbeing. The healing energy of the crystals merges with the body's energy fields, promoting harmony and balance. The similarities between crystals and the human body allow the cells of the body to communicate with each other, creating a transfer of energy and allowing the innate intelligence of the body to heal itself. Crystal healing is actually a science and works within a law of physics, the law of resonance, which states 'like energy attracts like energy'. This is why, when we are in the presence of crystals, they assist us in aligning with the same healing energy that is within.

Through our lives we experience many challenges that we sometimes misinterpret, which then creates much pain, hurt and fear, and we tend to shut off from ourselves and those around us. This process can start to create suppressed emotions within our energy field that can lay dormant, creating unwanted behavioural patterns in our lives. This imbalance in our energy body can eventually create disease within the physical body. These suppressed emotions, old patterns and belief systems are stored in our energy fields and become our emotional baggage. This can then create the feeling that we are not whole. The illusion of separation from our source starts to take place as we begin to identify ourselves as our issues instead of our true essence and divinity.

Crystals create a sacred, safe space for us to discard these old, suppressed emotions and unwanted patterns from our fields. Crystals know they are pure love and light of the universe. They gently assist us in connecting our higher selves with our pure essence as we align to the love and order of the universe, allowing transformation and deep healing to occur. The crystal vibration resonates with the energy in the body and the auric field, and the imbalance rises as a memory of the past. As we are held in the vibration of love and truth and with our hearts open, we are able to expand our awareness to see the truth within these experiences, and are given an opportunity to accept and release the issue. We move out of the old way of being and receive the blessings and gifts from such an experience. We surrender and set ourselves free from the chains of our old perception as we move deeper into our hearts and accept, love and nurture more aspects of our selves. This process creates a deep connection between our heart and soul, and an opportunity to look deeply into the inner self with unconditional love and trust.

From my own experience of healing I have come to understand that our most powerful gifts are hidden beneath our fears in those places that we feel uncomfortable in. Some call this place the shadow. I believe that this is where our power lies and our true gifts are revealed. There is always a blessing with a painful challenge — we just have to have the courage to look for it. This is a sacred process of healing and, when truly understood and felt in the heart, allows us much growth and an expanded awareness of ourselves that creates deep transformation and awakening. It creates much gratitude for life and allows us to know and accept ourselves completely. This healing journey makes us who we are, and creates great strength and courage of spirit.

Crystals and the past

Numerous cultures throughout history have harnessed the powerful energies of crystals. As far back as Atlantis, crystals have been respected, understood and recognised as energetic templates of divine knowledge and wisdom. The Atlanteans were from an advanced civilisation that used crystals in various forms for healing, gaining universal knowledge and spiritual awakening. They understood the forces that are generated by crystals and worked within these energetic laws to benefit their people.

In Australia the Aboriginal peoples would connect to certain crystals to assist in entering the Dreamtime.

Native Americans also understood crystals and their vast range of magical properties. They viewed them as among their most sacred possessions. Native Americans used the energetic properties of Quartz crystals to amplify and strengthen their own healing abilities and their connection to Mother Earth.

In preparation for entering into spiritual initiations the ancient Egyptians would grind crystals such as Lapis Lazuli and Carnelian to wear as makeup to assist in this process. Crystals have been found entombed with Egyptian mummies as part of the customary practice that assisted the dead to travel safely into the afterlife.

In South America, Peru and Mexico, several crystal skulls have been discovered. The most famous of these is the Mitchell-Hedges skull, which was found in the Mayan temples in Mexico. It is believed the skull assists humanity in our collective awakening and our journey into oneness.

Crystals and the modern world

It is very exciting that modern day sciences are beginning to understand the vast properties of crystals and their energy, and how we can utilise these powerful properties. Crystals play a huge role in our lives and are utilised in various ways. Crystals are found in many different machines that run our technology. They are used in computers to hold the memory, are found in our watches to keep the time and are even found in our television sets. The techno world would not exist today if it was not for the Crystal Kingdom because most of our modern technology is run on crystal energy in some form or another.

Crystals are being increasingly used for their healing purposes in modern medicine. Silicon crystal chips are used in pacemakers and rubies are used in surgical lasers. Crystals are also used in natural medicines by extracting the healing energies from the crystal into water for use as a base for medicines called gem essences or elixirs.

CLEANSING AND ENERGISING CRYSTALS

It is essential to cleanse and energise your crystals on a regular basis for several reasons. Science has proven that crystals store and retain energy so it is important that you clear the energy from them to keep your crystals clear and vibrant. Crystals come from deep within the Earth and when we remove them from their natural environment they lose their potent energy, so we are required to charge them back to their natural state.

Cleansing re-energises the crystal and ensures it is functioning at its full potential, clearing any previous energies, such as other people's thoughts and emotions. You will intuitively know when it is time to cleanse your crystals because they may look and feel dull in energy, or you may even pick up other energies radiating from the crystals.

Crystals amplify the light within. The more love you share with them, the more love and light they radiate back to you. I personally recommend you cleanse and charge your crystals at least once a month. Cleansing and charging your crystals before and after each healing is very important.

Cleansing methods

Following are some of the many ways and processes used to charge and cleanse crystals. Remember, there is no right or wrong way to cleanse and charge your crystals. Make sure to tune in to and work with the process that feels most effective for you. The most important aspect of this process is to set a strong intention of cleansing, then apply your specific cleansing technique.

Water

Certain crystals are sensitive to water, usually those with striations or with soft or brittle textures. Use other methods to cleanse and charge these crystals.

✦ **Salt water** — Crystals love a visit to the beach. Dip your crystals into the sea. Be sure to rinse them with fresh water afterwards and dry them with a cloth. The salt assists in dissolving any unwanted energies.

✦ **Fresh water** — When cleansing crystals with fresh water, choose water that is energetically clear, such as rain water or water in nature. If you are unable to find these water sources, use bottled or distilled water. If you choose tap water, clear the water energetically with Reiki, clearing pendants or pure intention before you use it. Natural springs, waterfalls and streams — Place your crystals in nature to assist in their rejuvenation.

Sound

Crystals enjoy a sound bath because it brings the crystal back to its natural vibration. It turns the crystal on and amplifies its energy.

✦ **Voice** — Hold the intention of cleansing your crystal and allow yourself to move into a space of clarity. Tone directly into your crystal, giving the sound the freedom to emanate whatever tone manifests. This method will powerfully align your energy with the vibration of the crystal.

✦ **Tuning forks, Tibetan bells and bowls, and crystal bowls** — Sound the instrument while moving it over the crystal with the intention of clearing and energising the crystal.

✦ **Music** — Soft, high vibrational and spiritual music playing in a room will cleanse and energise your crystals.

Other cleansing techniques

✦ **Smudging** — The most effective herbs or incense for smudging are sage and frankincense. Burn in a bowl, creating cleansing smoke, and set the intention of cleansing as you blow the smoke over the crystals.

✦ **Visualisation** — Create a simple visualisation of a waterfall and see your crystals being cleansed under the crystal clear water.

✦ **Light** — Visualise and invoke golden or violet light and see this light penetrate into your crystal, setting the intention of cleansing.

✦ **Reiki** — Crystals love Reiki energy. You can cleanse and charge your crystals by placing a clearing or charging symbol into them.

Energising methods

Many methods can be used to energise or charge your crystals.

✦ **Sunlight** — The sun will charge your crystal with masculine energy qualities such as strength, power and assertiveness. Crystals originate from Mother Earth and usually don't like a lot of direct sunlight Too much sunlight can discolour your crystals and heat changes the chemical structure. Charge your crystals in direct sunlight for no more than a few hours.

✦ **Moonlight** — Crystals love a beautiful moon bath. Just like us, crystals are affected strongly by the phases of the moon due to the water element that exists within us and crystals. You can place your crystal under any phase of the moon, with the full moon being the most potent. The magnetic charge and pull on the Earth during this time assists in energising the crystal. It is best to lay the crystals on the Earth under the moon. However, if you live in a place where this is not possible, you can still energise your crystals by moonlight by placing them in a pot plant next to a window or on a balcony under direct moonlight. The moon will charge your crystals with feminine energies such as compassion, healing and nurturing.

✦ **Energy grids** — Energy grids are vortexes of light where the energy is high, pure and constantly charging. You can create your own grid, or work with copper pyramids. Place the crystals within the grid where they will be charged with universal energy.

✦ **Mother Earth** — Crystals originally come from the Earth. Placing your crystal back into the Earth will fully restore its natural energy and beauty. Make sure to connect with the crystal to find out how long it would like to be left in the Earth. A short part of a day can restore your crystal to its full potential; however, each crystal is unique.

+ **Other crystals** — Crystal clusters and geode caves still remain in their natural state and continuously recharge themselves, so they are ideal for recharging other crystals. Place your crystal into a crystal geode cave or onto a crystal cluster.

+ **Energy pendants** — Several energy pendants designed to clear and recharge energies are available on the market.

CONNECTING TO YOUR CRYSTALS

Crystals invite us all to connect deeply with their essence and energy so they can assist us on our healing journey. Each crystal has a special and unique message, medicine and energy to share with us.

The word 'crystal' comes from the Greek word, krustallos, meaning ice or frozen light. Crystals are pure light and energy, and light is a medium of information. Each crystal is a channel of Divine Love and wisdom from the universe and the Earth with knowledge to impart.

Crystals are a divine reflection of our soul and mirror back to us the love that is our pure essence and true state of being. Crystals share the truth of our existence and inner knowing, and assist us in bringing this awareness to the surface for us to receive and believe in ourselves.

Creating the time and space to connect to your crystals individually will bring your understanding of crystals and your own healing journey to a whole new level, allowing you to deepen your understanding of these amazing gifts from the Earth. The following guide will help you in your practice.

+ Gently close your eyes.
+ Bring your awareness to your breath, the in breath and the out.
+ Allow yourself to let go and relax.

+ With each breath you take you become more and more relaxed.
+ Become aware now of your own heartbeat.
+ Drop deeply into this loving vibration, dropping deeper and deeper.
+ Feel yourself journey deep into the heart of the Earth.
+ Feel your heart begin to merge and beat as one with our divine Earth Mother.
+ Open and receive the love and healing that is created from this sacred connection.
+ Now place your crystal on your heart centre, feeling deeply into its heartbeat.
+ Breathe in this loving healing vibration, as your heart beats as one with this powerful medicine of the Earth.
+ Now invoke and call upon the spirit and Deva of this beautiful crystal. As the Deva enters into your sacred space, it showers you in this healing light and crystal love.
+ Open fully to receive this blessing from the Crystal Kingdom.
+ Allow this crystal energy to flow from your heart into every cell of your being.
+ Radiate this healing vibration out into your auric field as you connect deeply, becoming one with your crystal.
+ Work now gently with your breath.
+ Inhale deeply. On the inhale, your crystal pulsates and radiates its loving, healing energy back into your heart. On the exhale send love from your heart and offer this love into the heart of your crystal.
+ Breathe like this for a few minutes, sharing this sacred healing space together as this loving being of the Crystal Kingdom assists you in activating and awakening the powerful healing energy that lies within.
+ Become aware of how you feel and what you are experiencing as you connect deeply to this sacred medicine.
+ Open now to receive any wisdom or messages this crystal has to share.

+ Take a moment to thank your crystal for sharing this sacred space and for all the healing you have received.
+ Know that you are one with this loving gift from Mother Earth and there is no separation.
+ Bring your awareness back into the room.
+ Call all aspects of your self into the here and now.
+ Gently open your eyes.

Crystal Devas

All crystals have Devas and Master Devas that share the same energetic vibration. The crystal Deva is the higher self or pure consciousness of the physical crystal. I believe the Deva of the crystal is the crystal, they are not separate. Just as we have Guides and Angels who assist us in our journey on Earth, crystals also have beings of light that oversee their evolution.

It is very important when we align and work with these powerful healing tools that we also honour and connect with their Devas and consciousness. They are alive and constantly calling for us to recognise their presence and offering realisation of our divine self through their reflection.

We can invoke and call upon the Devas of the crystals at any time for direction, guidance and healing. The Devas will show themselves to us in forms that we recognise, such as Angels, butterflies, dragons, fairies, goddesses, faces, shapes and symbols, and anything we can imagine.

PROGRAMMING CRYSTALS

It is scientifically proven that Quartz crystals store, absorb, send, receive and amplify energy. When offering or sending a thought or intent into a crystal it is possible for it to receive and store this energy and information. Once the crystal retains the thought or energy it has the ability to amplify and project it back to us, acting as a great tool of manifestation. Programming a crystal involves having the intention to use it for a particular purpose, such as meditation, affirmations, prayers, mantras, all types of healing, storing information, creating abundance, inner peace, Divine Love, truth, and anything your heart desires. Working with the intention of transformation will shift your energy and expand your conscious awareness.

The law of intention is a powerful process and applies when working with crystals. To program a crystal, simply choose an intention aligning to energy that you would like to store within the crystal. The crystal will store and retain your intention, aligning itself with this energy, amplifying it and sending it back into your energy field. This will assist you in manifesting the positive outcome into your life.

Crystals act as amplifiers and tools in creating an opportunity for you to align with your intention. However, it is important to understand that it is you who allows this process to occur. To choose an intention I suggest you tune into where you are presently in your life and select an intention that will assist you in your healing and transformation in the now.

Crystals already hold their own intentions and healing vibrations; however, in the process of programming we are fine tuning and aligning the energy personally to assist in specific healing and transformation. You do not have to program all your crystals. This process and information is here for those who would like to tune in and do their own personal healing, taking the next step and working consciously with the Crystal Kingdom. By programming a crystal you are calling this crystal consciousness into your life as a new guide in your healing journey. The crystal you program will become like a new best friend, here to guide, support and love you on your path.

Clear Quartz crystals are the most effective to use for programming because their properties allow programming to occur more readily than any other crystal group. I recommend that you work with a cleansed and charged crystal and with one intention at a time. The greater the stillness you embody when programming, the deeper the programming will penetrate into your crystal. Your intention will usually stay held within the crystal for up to a month. You may not require to work with the intention for that long. Once you have embodied your desired intention it is time to choose and work with another one. When reprogramming your crystal, clear and charge it before you infuse it with any more thoughts.

You can also program a crystal that is not in your physical environment. Energy travels through time and space, which allows you to send thoughts, intentions and feelings to the particular crystal through the cosmos. All that is required is to set an intention and visualise the crystal you would like to program.

The most important part of this process of programming is to make sure you deeply connect with the energy and vibration of the crystal you will be working with. Once a deep connection is established it is much easier for the crystal to receive your program because the connection works as a tunnel for the information and energy to move through, allowing the programming to be received. In the last section of the book you were guided on how to connect with your crystal so you are now familiar with this process.

Following is a step-by-step guide to programming your crystals.

Programming your crystal

+ Choose the crystal you would like to program.
+ Choose an intention that you would like to program into your crystal.
+ Visualise a beautiful golden light beaming down from the heavens.
+ Draw this magnificent golden light in through your crown chakra at the top of your head.
+ Allow this divine light of the universe to flow down deeply into your heart.

✦ Feel your heart expand as it receives this love from the divine source.

✦ Now send this golden light down through your body and out through the bottom of your feet.

✦ Allow yourself to be a conduit and channel for this divine light.

✦ Feel this golden light flow into each and every cell of your being.

✦ Now send this golden light down deeply into the Earth, down into the heart of the planet. Mother Earth becomes aware of your presence and sends you her loving, nurturing, healing energy.

✦ Breathe this energy up through your feet, up through your body and deeply into your heart.

✦ Bring your awareness now to your heart chakra, breathing in the divine light of the universe and drawing the healing energy up from the Earth at the same time.

✦ Allow this light of Heaven and Earth to touch you deeply and fully as you merge as one.

✦ Place your crystal in your right hand.

✦ Send this golden light of the universe down your arms and into your hands, and offer this golden light to your crystal.

✦ Your crystal receives this light, expands, and starts to vibrate and resonate in the palm of your hand.

✦ Now draw the energy of your crystal from your hand, up your arm and deeply into your heart.

✦ From your heart allow this energy to flow into every single cell.

✦ Now call upon the spirit and Deva of this powerful crystal to enter into the room and bathe you in this crystal vibration.

✦ Open and receive as you start to become one with this crystal energy.

✦ Now invoke the energy of your intention, prayer or mantra.

✦ Draw this awareness into your heart and your mind.

✦ Become your intention, feel your intention, see your intention.

✦ Drop deeply into this energy as you resonate at the same vibration as your intention.

+ Now place your crystal on your third eye.
+ Breathe the energy of this crystal deeply into your third eye point, as you feel your inner vision and sight expand.
+ Spend the next few minutes sending and offering your intention from your heart up into your third eye and into your crystal.
+ Repeat this three times.
+ See your intention, experience your intention and feel this powerful intention anchor deeply into the inner chamber of your crystal.
+ Your crystal expands to receive your powerful intention, prayer or mantra with ease and grace.
+ Now place your crystal on your heart chakra and send it love from deep within.
+ Seal your intention with Divine Love.
+ Place your crystal in your left hand, allowing yourself to receive your intention back into your energy field and heart chakra, completing the cycle of giving and receiving.
+ Open to receive this divine blessing. This crystal now holds the sacred vibration of your powerful intent as it amplifies this energy back to you, assisting you to manifest this into your life and reality. This crystal is now like a new best friend, here to share this sacred journey with you.
+ Take a moment to thank your crystal for sharing this sacred space with you.
+ Now bring yourself back, calling all aspects of yourself back into the room into this present moment.
+ Gently open your eyes.

You have now created a deep, sacred union with your crystal, which is now dedicated to assist you on your healing journey. To deepen this process, carry and sleep with your crystal, keeping it in your energy field.

Following are suggested affirmations to program into your crystals.

- ✦ I am inspired.
- ✦ I am empowered.
- ✦ I do what I love and I love what I do.
- ✦ My awareness is constantly expanding and my conscious is awakening.
- ✦ I am attuned to my divine will.
- ✦ I am in divine alignment with my higher self.
- ✦ I am joy.

LOVE
- ✦ I am open to giving and receiving love.
- ✦ I am at peace with myself and with the universe.
- ✦ I am a radiant, conscious being of love and light.
- ✦ I feel gratitude for all I am and all I do.
- ✦ I am aligned with my truth in every moment.
- ✦ I am love and love is me.

HEALTH
- ✦ Radiant green healing light fills every cell of my being with love and healing.
- ✦ I am happy, healthy and whole.
- ✦ Every cell in my body is happy.

PROSPERITY
- ✦ I am abundant in all aspects of my life.
- ✦ Abundance radiates in every cell of my being.
- ✦ Abundance flows into my life with ease and grace.

CRYSTAL GRIDS

Creating crystal grids is as simple as laying crystals in a specific pattern to create an energy vortex, amplifying the healing energy of the crystals and your chosen intention. You can place grids in your home, around your garden, in your healing room, on the earth and around your vision board to amplify the crystals' healing energy for a specific purpose. Crystal grids are a powerful way to use crystal energy to amplify their vast healing properties. Crystals' energy is lessened when they are removed from the Earth and creating grids is a powerful way of amplifying and keeping crystals charged.

The grids create potent energy vortexes that amplify the crystal energy, constantly charging each other and the crystals in the grid. The crystal grid amplifies the energy of the crystal that is placed in the centre, which is called the anchor crystal, creating an amplified energy field around the grid and out into the physical environment.

You can use various formations to create grids. I have come to understand that working with the sacred symbol and structure of the six-pointed star and laying the crystals in this form creates a very powerful and potent grid and vortex. The six-pointed star formation has been used for thousands of years and has the qualities of bringing spirit energy and higher vibrational frequencies into the physical plane. This makes the six-pointed star the perfect formation to use for grid work.

Placing a crystal in the centre, then laying the six-terminated crystals (crystals with a point at the end) in the six-pointed star formation and activating the grid or formation will create your grid and energy vortex. Once the grid is activated it will constantly amplify and charge itself as the anchor crystal builds energy and spreads out from the grid, allowing the healing energy and specific intention of the grid to fill the whole environment in a very powerful and potent way.

Grids can also be programmed by placing and projecting an intention into the grid. The crystals in the grid store the intention and continuously amplify it, making it a powerful manifestation tool. You do not have to program all your grids; you can simply activate the grid to amplify the energies of the anchor crystal and specific grid choice.

Always work with cleansed and charged crystals. Once you activate the grid the energy will continue to amplify until the grid crystals have been moved or knocked. When establishing your grids I suggest you create a sacred space because this is a powerful ritual and the energy you create will manifest into your grid. Make sure to do this when you are feeling centred and calm because the crystals will pick up on your energy and amplify it.

Creating your own crystal grids

+ **In healing rooms** — You can place your grid under your healing table, or touching the sides of the wall, so you are actually inside the grid. Choose which healing energy you would like to create and select the crystals that resonate to that frequency. Rose Quartz and Amethyst are great crystals to place within your grids in a healing room because they will fill your sacred space with love and healing energy.

+ **In and around your home** — Place grids in different rooms of your home to create and amplify crystal energies. Blue Lace Agate and Blue Calcite are ideal to place in your lounge room because they create clear and peaceful communication. Creating a grid around your home will create an energy of peace and tranquillity.

+ **When charging crystals** — Create a grid and program it with the intention of cleansing and charging your crystals, then place your crystals inside the grid.

+ **When programming** — You can also program the grid with affirmations, mantras, prayers, or specific intentions to assist you in all areas of your life.

+ **When distance healing** — Work with healing crystals in the centre of the grid and place a photo or the name of the person you would like to send healing to under the crystal in the centre. Call upon the person's Guides and Angels to send healing energy into the grid and ask that the healing be for their highest good. See the person as already healed, perfect, whole and complete. Ask the higher self of the person to whom you are sending healing to let you know when to take down the grid.

✦ **Around vegetable gardens** — Plants receive the loving energies of crystals organically. Placing a grid around your garden will assist in the growth and health of your plants and vegetables.

✦ **Around vision boards** — Placing a grid around your vision board will strengthen the opportunity for you to manifest your dreams and goals.

✦ **Around healing centres** — Creating a grid buried in the Earth around your healing centre amplifies the energy of the sacred land and the intention of the healing space. This grid assists in keeping your sacred space clean and filled with divine energy of love from the universe.

✦ **For space clearing** — Setting the intention of clearing energies from a specific space and creating a grid to hold this intention creates a space clearing vortex.

✦ **For Earth healing** — Create crystal grids on the Earth to assist in the regeneration of our planet. Send mantras and prayers into your grid with the intention of healing the Earth.

Crystals you need to create a grid

✦ Six Clear Quartz terminator points (single or double pointed) are required to create a grid in the shape of a six-pointed star.

✦ Place your chosen crystal in the centre (this is the anchor crystal). This crystal will create the specific energy you would like amplified by your grid.

✦ Use a wand or small Clear Quartz single terminator point to activate the grid.

The larger the crystal, the more energy the grid will amplify. When you have activated the six-pointed star grid you can add more crystals to the grid, creating a mandala, in any shape or form. Remain open to becoming a channel for where the crystals would like to lay in the grid. This is a very intuitive process.

Grid activation

+ Start by creating a sacred space, calling in your Guides and Angels, and Devas of the crystals. You may also like to invoke the four elements and directions, Mother Earth and Divine Spirit.
+ Lay your six Clear Quartz terminated crystals in the shape of a six-pointed star, with the terminations pointing inwards.
+ Place your desired crystal (anchor crystal) in the centre and place your wand crystal or point in your hand.
+ Visualise golden light streaming down from the cosmos into your crystal grid and then down into Mother Earth. Connect to the Earth and visualise this energy moving up into your grid as your grid becomes connected and grounded into the Earth.
+ Call upon the golden light of the universe. Visualise this light streaming down into your crown chakra and then down into Mother Earth as you become a conduit. Connect to Mother Earth and breathe her energy up into your heart. Now breathe the golden light down from the universe and into your heart. Breathe these two energies into your heart centre at the same time.
+ Set your mind intention to activate the grid. If you are programming your grid, now is the time to set your intention for your program.
+ Now visualise the light and love from your heart and direct this energy into your wand, then into the grid.
+ Place your wand point over the anchor crystal in the centre.
+ Move the wand from the anchor crystal, connecting to one of the crystals on the outside of the grid, drawing a straight line.
+ Visualise the energy lines connecting to and from each crystal.
+ Continue to activate the grid by following the six-pointed star lines, moving from the outside crystal to the crystal next to it. Now

make your way back to the anchor crystal, then move back down the same line you just created to the same crystal on the outside. Connect to the crystal to the left in the six-pointed star, then draw the energy back into the centre crystal. Follow this format until you have activated the whole grid, working clockwise and finishing in the centre.

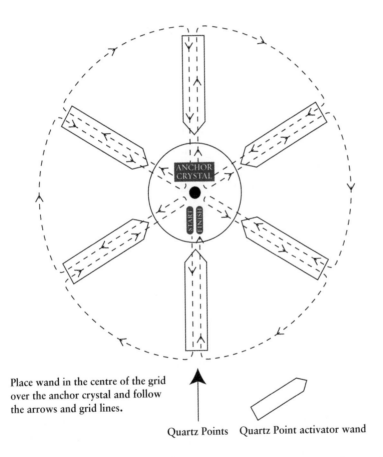

Place wand in the centre of the grid over the anchor crystal and follow the arrows and grid lines.

Quartz Points   Quartz Point activator wand

+ Visualise the energies streaming upwards out of the central crystal, spiralling the energy upwards.
+ Now using your voice or any other type of instrument, sound into the grid with the intention to activate and integrate the grid.

Note: A good way to keep your mind clear while doing the activation is to chant this healing invocation: 'I am a clear and pure channel, love is my guide'. Or you could chant Ohm Shanti, which means 'peace'.

You can add extra crystals to the grid by placing them in the centre, making sure you don't knock any of the crystals because that will create a break in the circuit and you will have to activate the grid again. You can also place more Quartz lasers on the outside of the grid, pointing outwards to direct the grid's energies out. And you can place a circle of Hematite around the outside of the grid to ground the energies.

CRYSTAL ESSENCES

Crystal essences are extremely powerful energetic medicines that have been used for thousands of years. The crystal essence is created when the vibration and energy of the crystal are transferred into water. Water stores this crystal healing energy, which is then amplified by the homeopathic process. A mother essence is created and from the mother essence another essence is created, which is the correct dosage and is taken as drops under the tongue. The crystal essence is absorbed through the tissue of the mouth and enters into the physical, emotional, mental and spiritual energetic bodies, where it promotes balance and healing. The crystal energy moves through the physical body into each cell, inviting the body to align with the crystal energy's natural healing process.

Crystal healing works within the laws of physics — in this case, the law of attraction. When the body receives the pure vibration and Earth medicine of the crystal energy, it invites and allows the body to align with natural healing energy that already exists within the body, aligning with the healing energy of the universe as balance is created and deep healing occurs. Each crystal resonates its unique healing vibration and invites transformation of any issues that align to this specific vibration, releasing the old and making way for the new.

Creating a crystal essence is a very personal experience and can be done in a variety of ways. The most important aspect of this process is your intention. I prefer to connect to my crystal and work with its energy before I create the essence. In this way my intention for the essence becomes a real experience. Be sure to take a whole, complete dosage (two to three weeks) after making your essence to finalise the integration process before you share it with others. It is also very important that when you create and birth your essences you are in an open, loving space. Remember you are working with energy medicine and the energy you are feeling while making your essence will be transferred into your elixir.

When making crystal essences it is essential to create a sacred space by conducting a ceremony, because this is a sacred ritual. Call in and ask for assistance from your Guides, Angels, Crystal Devas, the moon, the sun, the four elements, the four directions, totems and all the beings that are assisting you in this process.

It is possible to work with more than one crystal in your mother essence at a time. However, to create more options when making your daily dosage mix it is best to make the essences separately using individual crystals. For example, if you want to make a chakra clearing essence with seven crystals that represent each chakra, it is best to use the seven crystals in separate mother essences because this will give you more freedom to create different combinations in the future. If you were to use all seven crystals in the one mother essence it would restrict you to using the essence only for a chakra clearing essence. If you create seven individual mother essences, you can create the chakra clearing essence by putting a drop of each essence in your daily dosage bottle. That way you are getting all the crystals in your daily dosage bottle and still have the freedom to use the mother essences for other purposes and vibrational mixes.

Note: When making your essence it is very important that the crystal does not sit in the jar with the water in it because some crystals are not suitable to take into the physical body. Place the crystal in another jar inside the bowl. The energy will still be infused into the water; however, the physical properties will not be transmitted into the essence.

How to make mother essence

+ Choose the crystal or crystals that will hold and create your desired medicine or healing vibration for your essence.
+ As you are working with pure energy, make sure that all the utensils used to make the essence are cleansed energetically. You can do this by placing all your tools in a crystal grid.
+ Set an intention for your essence and tune into your crystal's healing energy.
+ Place the crystal inside a glass jar and place this jar into a glass bowl or Quartz crystal bowl full of purified water, ensuring your bowl or jar has a seal.
+ Place the essence in a crystal grid on the earth or in nature.
+ Conduct your ceremony as you call in assistance from the spirit realm and set your intention for the essence.
+ Leave the essence under the moon for three nights — the night before the full moon, the night of the full moon and the following night. The essence will now be ready to bottle. Two-thirds fill a 500 mL amber bottle with the essence. You can use the leftover essence to water your plants, give to your animals, place in the bath, or create crystal sprays.
+ Add at least one-third brandy to two-thirds essence and shake well. Brandy preserves your crystal essence. Note: Glycerin can be used instead of alcohol to preserve the essence; use it in the same quantity as the brandy.
+ Label the bottle with the following details: intention of essence, crystal used, date and moon phase.
+ Store the mother essence in a dark, dry place and ensure it does not touch other essences.

✦ Keep the crystal with the mother essence, touching the bottle, until it is finished, because it helps to hold the energy.

The mother essence will last around two years. When a film starts to form in the bottom of the jar throw it out, because this is bacteria.

How to make a daily dosage bottle

✦ Fill a 25 ml amber eyedropper bottle with two-thirds purified water and one-third brandy.
✦ Add seven drops of the mother essence.
✦ Label the bottle with the intention and the crystal used.
✦ To activate the essence, tap on the palm of the hand seven times.
✦ Take seven drops three times a day under the tongue.

Caffeine, alcohol, tobacco, mints, menthol, garlic and strong perfume block crystal essences, so avoid these substances half an hour before and after taking your essence.

CRYSTALS AND CHAKRAS

Chakras are centres of energy and consciousness within our energy body. Hundreds of chakras make up our energy field; however, we commonly work with seven main chakras. They are our main focal points of life energy. The chakras indicate our evolution spiritually, emotionally, mentally and physically. When we nourish our chakras on a regular basis they begin to radiate a brilliant light that creates balance on all levels in all of our bodies — the physical, emotional, mental and spiritual. Each chakra relates to different aspects of our life and each has a different colour and vibration. When the chakras are out of balance it can create disharmony in our day-to-day life.

It is very important when working with healing that we understand the chakra system because this is where most of our energetic blockages are held. When we understand the chakras and what they represent it is easier for us to identify with the issues that are creating imbalances and where they are held or stored. This allows for more understanding and knowledge of how we can assist people in releasing and dissolving unwanted energy and balancing the chakras.

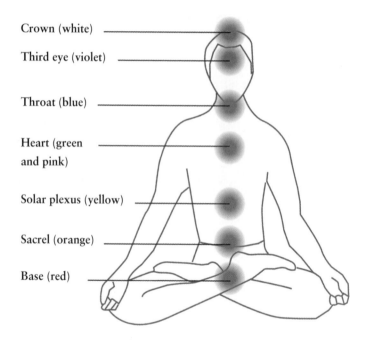

Crown (white)

Third eye (violet)

Throat (blue)

Heart (green and pink)

Solar plexus (yellow)

Sacrel (orange)

Base (red)

Different crystals align to and bring balance to each individual chakra, although some crystals relate to more than one chakra. The next section introduces you to the relationship between the chakras and the aligning crystals, and later in the book I introduce advanced chakra layouts.

Following is a simple breakdown of the aspects of our lives each chakra relates to, so you can start to get a deeper understanding of how this system works and relates to healing.

Base chakra

Colour: Red
Relates to:

+ Security and stability
+ Grounding
+ Survival
+ Instinct
+ Money
+ Material needs
+ Ancestors

Crystals associated with the base chakra are Black Obsidian, Red Jasper, Hematite, Shungite, Black Tourmaline, Smoky Quartz, Petrified Wood, Goethite, Pyrite, Stibnite, Agate, Amber, Apophylite, Chiastolite, Eudialyte, Apache Tears, Aragonite, Jet, Brown Tourmaline, Serpentine, Bloodstone, Mookite, Shaman and Boji Stones™, and Cuprite.

Sacral chakra

Colour: Orange
Relates to:

+ Desires
+ Appetites
+ Addictions
+ Creativity
+ Relationships
+ Karmic patterns
+ Sexuality and sensuality
+ Community, family and tribe

Crystals associated with the sacral chakra are Carnelian, Brown Tourmaline, Rutilated Quartz, Shiva Lingams, Tiger's Eye, Fire Agate, Bixbite, Crocoite, Ruby, Red Tourmaline, Agate, Amber, Apache Tears, Aragonite, Apophylite, Bloodstone, Eudialyte Cuprite, Jet, Moonstone, Serpentine, Mookite, Orpiment and Smoky Quartz.

Solar plexus chakra

Colour: Yellow
Relates to:

+ Empowerment
+ Confidence
+ Self-discipline
+ Free will
+ Self-esteem
+ Inner strength
+ Courage

Crystals associated with the solar plexus are Sunstone, Mookite, Chrysocolla, Golden Calcite, Citrine, Heliodor, Chrysanthemum Stone, Rhodonite, Amazonite, Ametrine, Brazilianite, Cacoxenite, Chrysoberyl, Fluorite, Tiger's Eye, Orpiment, Pyromorphite, Eudialyte and Sodalite.

Heart chakra

Colour: Green and pink
Relates to:

+ Unconditional love
+ Love of self
+ Compassion
+ Forgiveness
+ Acceptance
+ Nurturing
+ Receiving
+ Intimacy
+ Joy, laughter and happiness

Crystals that are associated with the heart are Rose Quartz, Green Adventerine, Kunzite, Rhodochrosite, Malachite, Chrysocolla, Chrysoprase, Diamond, Hiddenite, Morganite, Nirvana Quartz, Pink

Tourmaline, Green Tourmaline, Watermelon Tourmaline, Prehnite, Diopside, Dioptase, Emerald, Jade, Peridot, Sugilite, Ocean Jasper, Herkimer Diamond, Serpentine, Ajoite, Angelite, Green Apatite, Turquoise, Aquamarine, Celestite, Chrysoberyl, Fluorite, Larimar, Moonstone, Pyromorphite, Vivianite.

Throat chakra

Colour: Blue
Relates to:
+ Speaking your truth
+ Communication
+ Aligned to soul purpose
+ Expression
+ Creativity

Crystals associated with the throat are Blue Lace Agate, Aquamarine, Blue Kyanite, Ajoite, Dumortierite, Larimar, Sodalite, Blue Tourmaline, Turquoise and Vivianite.

Third eye chakra

Colour: Violet
Relates to:
+ Clarity and awareness
+ Deepening intuition
+ Visualisation
+ Spiritual insight
+ Dreams and visions

Crystals associated with the third eye are Amethyst, Azurite, Lapis Lazuli, Fluorite, Lepidolite, Tanzanite, Ametrine, Blue Apatite, Charoite, Labradorite, Natrolite, Phenacite, Purpurite, Shattuckite Pyrite and Blue Tourmaline.

Crown chakra

Colour: White
Relates to:

+ Union with higher self
+ I am presence
+ Connection with source
+ Divine knowledge and wisdom
+ Spiritual awareness

Crystals associated with the crown are Clear Quartz, Calcite, Selenite, Angelite, Cinnabar, Danburite, Libyan Tektite, Moldavite, Pietersite, Scolecite, Tektite, Amazonite, Chiastolite, Apophyllite, Blue Apatite, Brazilianite, Cacoxenite, Celestite, Charoite, Dumortierite, Herkimer Diamond, Labrodorite, Lapis Lazuli, Natrolite, Phenacite, Purpurite, Rutilated Quartz and Shattuckite

ALIGNING AND CONNECTING TO THE SEVEN MAIN CHAKRA CRYSTALS

For the next process you are required to work with the following seven crystals. If you are unable to purchase these crystals you can call on the Deva and invoke the energy with your intention. However, it is ideal to work with the physical crystals the first time you experience this process.

Each crystal has its own vibration and medicine; however, how this energy interacts with you is unique to each individual. This exercise is used to empower and encourage you to connect to each of the crystals and start to become aware of how each specific vibration and energy interacts with you.

The following crystals relate strongly to each chakra, bringing healing and balance. As you go through this process you will be actively clearing and balancing your chakras and energy field. Work with one crystal at a time in a quiet, relaxed environment. Become aware of how the crystal feels and how you feel as you embody its energy, connecting to and bringing out the energy that is within. This process allows for a deeper understanding of your chakras and how they relate in your life. Feel free to write your experience with the crystal in the blank section below each crystal for your own reference.

Base chakra — **Hematite** — metallic

Sacral chakra — **Carnelian** — brown to orange

Solar plexus chakra — **Citrine** — yellow or golden

Heart chakra — **Rose Quartz** — pink

Throat chakra — **Blue Lace Agate** — blue

Third eye chakra — **Amethyst** — purple

Crown chakra — **Selenite** — white

Mother Earth crystal Deva chakra meditation

The following meditation is for anyone looking for powerful transformation and healing in their lives through a deep connection to the Crystal Kingdom and Mother Earth.

As you take this meditation journey deep within the Earth you will be guided to open your heart to receive healing. You will experience a deep connection to yourself and the Earth, feeling a sense of balance, wellbeing, inner peace, relaxation and unconditional love, allowing you to feel more joy, abundance and empowerment in your life.

As you experience this powerful meditation of connecting deeply with yourself, Mother Earth and her powerful gifts of the Crystal Kingdom, you will feel your heart open, creating an opportunity for deep healing to take place. You will journey deep within the Earth, experiencing and receiving healing from seven magical crystal Devas, which will allow for clearing and balancing of your major chakras. Through this meditation you may experience a letting go of painful wounds of the past and an opportunity to dissolve any old patterns as the gentle, loving, healing energy of the crystals support you in your transformation.

To integrate and deepen the experience you can physically work with each crystal one at a time or all together. You may lay them on your chakras or simply have them in your hands during meditation. It is recommended you continue connecting to the crystals, keeping them in your presence, because they will assist in integrating any further healing. Know that you can enter back into the crystal healing cave any time you wish, calling upon the crystal Devas. Continue to deepen your connection with the Earth, enjoying more time in nature.

Meditation process

Gently close your eyes, bringing your awareness to your breath. Allow your breath to take you on a journey deep within, to the core of your being, into your own sacred space. With each breath that you take, feel yourself becoming more and more relaxed. As you let go of all thought, allow yourself to journey deeper and deeper within. Feel yourself gently dropping deeper as you bring your awareness to your heart chakra. Feel the love that you have deep within your heart as you enter into your own sacred space.

Find yourself now at the edge of a beautiful and mystical sacred forest. You can hear the birds in the trees and feel the sun shining down upon you. Feel the sun's warmth on your face. Your heart is filled with gratitude as you arrive in this divine and magical place. Allow yourself to be drawn into the forest. Feel the nature spirits of this healing land welcoming you as they offer to you their healing energy. Continue to walk and journey deeper into this sacred forest, allowing yourself to feel the spirits of the trees and the ancestors of the land. With each step that you take feel Mother Earth beneath your feet, supporting your every move. Feel her hold and nurture you as you open to receive her loving embrace.

You now arrive deep within the heart of this magical forest. As you look around become aware of an amazing ancient tree, hundreds of years old. Feel the spirit of this beautiful and powerful tree communicating with you; allow this time to receive and embrace her. You now realise that there's a hole in the trunk of this tree. This is an entry point for you to journey deep within Mother Earth. Climb inside the trunk and feel yourself gently begin to journey down into the Earth. Hold onto the roots of the tree as they assist you in moving deeper and deeper, feeling yourself being held and supported by the ancient tree as you drop gently into the Earth.

Feel the warmth deep within the Earth as you become aware of the sound and vibration of her heartbeat. Feel this healing heartbeat resonate through each of your cells, filling your soul with love and healing. Continue journeying further into the Earth as you feel a sense of wonder and awe for what you are about to experience. You look around and become aware that you have entered into a mystical crystal cave deep within the heart of our Earth Mother.

Feel the gentle waves of healing energy moving through you as you experience the enchantment and magic inside this amazing crystal cave. You become aware of a Quartz crystal bed lying in the centre of this cave, radiating pure light. You feel this energy inviting you to lie down upon this healing bed. Take a few moments to connect to this beautiful, loving, gentle energy as you surrender, allowing yourself to receive. This is your time to be nurtured and revitalised, as you lay upon your crystal healing bed deep within the heart of Mother Earth.

Slowly, one by one, seven majestic crystal Devas enter into your divine healing cave. These beings of light are here to share their transformational healing energy and wisdom with you as they assist you in activating, healing and balancing your chakras. Slowly each Deva moves over to you on your crystal healing bed, creating a sacred circle around you as they pulsate loving energies deep into your being.

The first Deva, the Deva of Hematite, places a Hematite crystal on your base chakra at the bottom of your spine. This divine being infuses loving, healing energy into this crystal as it expands and awakens, directing and offering this energy into your base chakra. Visualise the colour red and allow this vibration to flow deeply into your base, moving through your chakra. Feel this energy enter deeply, as you allow yourself to let go of any fear and insecurity in your life, allowing you to feel safe and protected here on Earth. Open and receive this healing energy, as you feel strong, grounded and connected to Mother Earth.

The next Deva, the Deva of Carnelian, places a Carnelian crystal on your sacral chakra, around your navel. This divine being infuses loving, healing energy into this crystal as it expands and awakens, directing and offering this energy into your chakra. Visualise the colour orange, allowing this vibration to flow deeply into your sacral chakra, moving through your chakra. Feel this energy enter deeply, allowing yourself to dissolve any emotional entanglements and suppressed emotions that no longer serve you, and feeling a sense of inner peace and tranquillity. Allow inspiration to rise from within your being as you activate your creativity and passion for life. This powerful, healing energy enters you fully, deepening your connection to your family, community and tribe.

The next Deva, the Deva of Citrine, places a Citrine crystal on your solar plexus, around your stomach. This divine being infuses loving, healing energy into this crystal as it expands and awakens, directing and offering this energy into your chakra. Visualise the colour yellow, allowing this vibration to flow deeply into your solar plexus, moving through your chakra. Feel this energy shower upon you. Let go of any issues around you, step into your power and follow your divine mission here on Earth. Experience a sense of confidence, worthiness and empowerment resonate from deep within your soul. Feel this healing energy deeply penetrate every cell of your being as you feel the joy and abundance of life.

The next Deva, the Deva of Rose Quartz, now places a Rose Quartz crystal on your heart chakra. This divine being infuses loving, healing energy into this crystal as it expands and awakens, directing and offering this energy into your chakra. Visualise the colour green, allowing this gentle, loving light to heal and nurture you. Feel the energy of unconditional love enter your heart, dissolving any old wounds and barriers. Allow the energy of Divine Love to flow gently into those inner chambers, hidden within your heart chakra, flowing within you as you feel safe and free to experience deep love for yourself and others.

The next Deva, the Deva of Blue Lace Agate, now places a Blue Lace Agate crystal on your throat chakra. This divine being infuses loving, healing energy into this crystal as it expands and awakens, directing and offering this energy into your chakra. Visualise the colour blue, allowing this vibration to flow deeply into your throat, moving through your chakra. Let yourself be showered in this healing energy as it dissolves any challenges around communication and expressing your divine truth. As the colour and vibration bathes and heals you, feel your throat chakra open and expand, allowing you to express yourself with ease and grace.

The next Deva, the Deva of Amethyst, places an Amethyst crystal on your third eye chakra. This divine being infuses loving, healing energy into this crystal as it expands and awakens, directing and offering this energy into your chakra. Visualise the colour violet, allowing this vibration to flow deeply into your third eye, moving through your chakra. Allow yourself to receive this healing energy, letting go of any limitations to your psychic abilities, spiritual sight and intuition. As the colour and vibration flows deeply into your third eye, feel your intuition deepen and your awareness expand, allowing you to experience clarity with each step that you take here on Earth.

The next Deva, the Deva of Selenite, places a huge Selenite rod at the top of your head, at your crown chakra. This divine being infuses loving, healing energy into this crystal as it expands and awakens, directing and offering this energy into your chakra. As you receive this healing light, allow yourself to open to the higher realms as you visualise vibrant white healing light flowing into your crown chakra, deepening your connection to spirit, the cosmos, your higher self and the oneness of all that is.

As you continue to lie on your crystal bed receiving this powerful healing, feel Mother Earth's nurturing energy flowing deep into your being. Tune in and feel her heartbeat resonate through every cell, allowing the energy of Mother Earth to hold you and to heal you. As the crystal energy continues to resonate into all your chakras, feel them come into balance and alignment with your higher self. Feel a sense of clarity, love, inner peace and wellbeing in your world.

It is now time to leave your sacred cave and give thanks to the Devas for sharing in your powerful healing. Know that you can return here at any time you like because this is your sacred healing cave, deep within the Earth. Start to make your way back up the roots of the beautiful ancient tree, feeling her wisdom and support as you journey all the way back up from the centre of the Earth.

You find yourself once again in the hollow trunk of the tree. As you climb from the tree take a moment to thank her, feeling the love and appreciation flow between you as you receive her Divine Love into your heart.

It is now time to leave this sacred land as you journey back through the magical forest. Feel supported by Mother Earth with each step you take as you journey back. The ancestors of this amazing sacred land bless and honour you as you slowly return.

Gently and very slowly move back into the room, back into this physical plane, as you call all aspects of self back into the here and now. It is now time to slowly open your eyes when you are ready.

CRYSTAL CHAKRA HEALING

Laying the crystals on the body in the area of the chakras allows alignment and balance to occur. The crystal vibration connects to our vibration and the law of resonance is activated, allowing us to open and surrender, and for healing to take place. Most of our energetic patterns and suppressed emotions can be held within the chakras. A simple balancing can create deep healing of these emotions and bring deep self-awareness, allowing for a greater sense of wellbeing in our lives.

Now you understand the chakras and have had your own experiences with the main chakra crystals, it is time to take this healing to the next level. You can do this very simple healing process on yourself or share it with others, working with the intention of balancing and energising the chakra system. You will be connecting to the crystals that you have just embodied from the last exercise. Note that it's important that you know your crystals and their energies before you assist another person in their healing. The following healing can also be done on yourself by laying the crystals on your chakras and taking yourself into a sacred healing space, allowing the crystals to work their magic.

Set an energetically clean, safe and nurturing space to facilitate your healing before you start. We are working with energy so cleanse the room with sage or some other form of clearing process to dissolve any unwanted energy that may be in the room. Make sure the room is comfortable as this will allow you to relax and open and receive a lot deeper. This can be achieved by lighting a candle and putting on some soft, relaxing music. Then take some time for yourself to go within and connect to your heart, relaxing your mind.

The most important thing to remember when sharing healing with others is to have an open heart and work with the energy of love and compassion. Remember to always set an intention that the healing is for the highest good of everyone involved. This allows the Divine Love of the universe to flow into your healing with a pure intention. We all have the gift of love and the essence of healing is love, so this means that we all have the gift of healing.

I believe healing is very much about supporting and sharing love with our fellow brothers and sisters on this planet. I believe anyone and everyone can facilitate healing by simply setting the sacred intention and allowing love and compassion to flow from the heart. I also believe if you are drawn to share healing space with others you have probably been a healer in another time. The first healing I ever facilitated was like a deep remembering and awakening of something I knew long ago. This sacred healing space sparked the deep wisdom and knowledge I have within. In saying this, it is important to listen to your own guidance and intuition during a healing, because this can be a great guide and tool for the healing to penetrate to a deeper level. The first time you do healing there is a good chance that you might not know how to listen to your inner guidance; however, like everything, the more you do something the more you will be open to and understand the process.

Healing is also about calling upon the loving beings in the other realms to support and guide us in our healing space; calling our Angels, loved ones who have passed, ascended masters, your totem spirit animals and other beings from the light who would like to be present. As you step into a healing space with others you become a channel and conduit of love from the universe, allowing the healing to flow through you. You do not have to make anything happen other than open your heart and send love to the person with whom you are facilitating the healing. The main essence of this healing is working with the crystals and their powerful healing medicine and energy. The crystals have an intelligence of their own and know exactly what healing to do once placed on the chakras as the law of attraction comes into play.

For now all you are required to do is follow the steps below to facilitate your healing, open your heart and enjoy the process of dancing with the healing energy of the Crystal Kingdom.

Facilitate your own chakra crystal healing

Following is a step-by-step guide on how to facilitate a simple yet powerful chakra balancing working with crystals, guiding you as you take your first step on the path of sharing the healing energy of the Crystal Kingdom with another person. Follow the steps below, but also be open to following your own intuition and guidance.

+ Always work with crystals that have been cleansed and charged.
+ Prepare the healing space and clear any unwanted energies in the room by burning sage or clearing intention.
+ Take a few moments to connect with your crystals and yourself.
+ Make sure you are both hydrated; drink plenty of water.
+ Lay the crystals on the allocated chakras.
  Base chakra (at the base of the spine) — place the crystal Hematite
  Sacral chakra (just beneath the belly button) — place the crystal Carnelian
  Solar plexus chakra (around the stomach area) — place the crystal Citrine
  Heart chakra (on the heart) — place the crystal Rose Quartz
  Throat chakra (on the throat area) — place the crystal Blue Lace Agate
  Third eye chakra (between the eyebrows) — place the crystal Amethyst
  Crown chakra (the top of the head) — place the crystal Selenite

+ Call upon your healing Guides, Angels and crystal Devas. Set the healing space by saying an invocation that allows you to open to divine healing energy from the universe (see below). Feel free to use your own invocation.

HEALING INVOCATION

I invoke the love of the divine universe within my heart
I am a clear and pure channel
Love is my guide

I invoke the love of the divine universe within my heart
I am a clear and pure channel
Love is my guide

I invoke the love of the divine universe within my heart
I am a clear and pure channel
Love is my guide

And I follow that LOVE

When you step into a sacred healing space you become a channel of healing energy, which is why it is important to call upon other helpers in the spirit world to guide the way.

Gently guide your client to close their eyes and focus on their breath as they move deeply into relaxation, allowing your client to open up and receive the energy.

Visualise golden light streaming down from the universe through your crown chakra, down into your heart, then direct this energy and offer it to the Earth. Expand the energy of love within your heart. Extend the loving energy down your arms, into your hands. This opens your heart so you can share this energy in the healing.

+ Place your hands over the crystals that lay on your client's chakras. With the intention of balancing the chakra, direct the crystal energy into the chakra point. You can also give Reiki or any other healing energy work that you are familiar with and aligned to.

Your focus on each crystal and your intention of balancing the chakra will activate and invoke the crystal energy. This energy is intelligent and knows what to do in the healing. You are the conduit that activates this consciousness and are a channel of love and light of the universe.

✦ Hold this space of healing with each chakra and crystal until you feel the energy disperse or release.

This can feel different for many people. You may feel the chakra sucking the energy from your hand, then suddenly stop. You may feel heat over the chakra, which then becomes cool. You may feel an energy shift, or move, inside you. The more you do these healings, the more you will feel the shift. The shift can also feel different each time you experience it. Remember to tune in and listen to your intuition.

✦ Start working on the base chakra and then work your way up to the crown.

✦ To finish the healing, guide your client gently back into the room by saying something like 'Calling all aspects of the self back into the room, into the physical. When you're ready, slowly open your eyes.'

✦ Ask your client to share their experience and take this time to listen and support with an open heart in unconditional love.

✦ Please share with your client any messages that you might have received from the universe, spirit or the crystal Devas in the healing.

During a healing you can experience a range of emotions and feelings, from inner peace and relaxation to sadness. Crystals can invoke many different experiences: each experience is individual and unique. Whatever may occur for you, remember it is perfect and it will take a little time to integrate. If you are feeling light-headed or floaty you are not grounded, so ensure you rub your feet and have something to eat.

Crystal healing and chakra balancing can take a few days to completely integrate. Emotions may surface in the days after the healing or even in the healing. Tears are a wonderful and powerful way of release, and for cleansing the old and making way for the new.

The physical and emotional bodies also require time out to rest and recuperate, so here are suggestions for nurturing the mind, body and soul after a healing.

+ Soak in an Epsom salts bath. Add essential oils to relax the mind, body and soul. Some great oils for relaxation are lavender, chamomile, geranium and sandalwood.
+ Take some time to walk in nature.
+ Take some time out to do something you love — some play time. Try writing, drawing, painting, swimming, hanging out with friends, or just hanging out with yourself.
+ Walk along the beach and swim in the ocean.

Advanced chakra crystal healing layouts

These powerful layouts have been created as a tool to delve deeper into the healing realms of the Crystal Kingdom. The advanced layouts are made of various different crystals working together, creating a potent and powerful healing energy that penetrates to a deeper healing level within the chakras. As we invite more crystals into the layout, we invoke and draw upon many different healing medicines and vibrations that create powerful transformation, awakening, balance and wellbeing. Following is an easy-to-understand guide to the crystals and their properties, the issues they can assist in healing in your life specific to each chakra and the benefits created by each crystal layout.

Having worked with and integrated the energy of the single crystals on the chakras, it is time to start working with and connecting to the advanced grids. Here, the single crystals are replaced by the advanced layouts. When laying the crystals on the chakras, tune into your intuition as to the formation to place them in. As long as the crystals are on the chakras, the crystal energy will flow to where it is required.

Base chakra crystal layout

This crystal layout assists in transforming issues of:

+ Abandonment
+ Physical abuse
+ Anxiety and depression
+ Lack of money
+ Poor focus
+ Ancestral karmic patterns
+ Unhealthy boundaries
+ Lethargy and lack of energy
+ Financial Issues
+ Disorders of the bowel and large intestine.
+ Disorders of the body such as bones, legs, feet and knees.

The crystal layout creates:

+ Trust
+ Appropriate boundaries
+ Prosperity
+ Stability
+ Energy
+ Connection to the Earth
+ Physical wellbeing
+ Vitality
+ Balance
+ Rejuvenation.

Crystals to use in this layout are:

+ Two Black Obsidian
+ Two Red Jasper
+ Two Hematite
+ Two Black Tourmaline
+ Two Smoky Quartz.

Properties of the crystals:
+ Black Obsidian: Dissolves destructive patterns in your life
+ Red Jasper: Draws up the healing energies of the Earth
+ Hematite: Grounds, cleanses, purifies and energises the physical body
+ Black Tourmaline: Transmutes and dissolves any stuck or dormant energies
+ Smoky Quartz: Transforms negative energy and thought forms, making you feel rejuvenated.

Sacral chakra crystal layout

This crystal layout assists in transforming issues of:
+ Addiction
+ Eating disorders
+ Blame and guilt
+ Emotional imbalance
+ Rejection
+ Family issues
+ Relationship issues
+ Fear of change
+ Anger
+ Sexual issues
+ Disorders of the reproductive system, spleen, bladder, large intestine, urinary system, menstrual difficulties, lower back pain, diarrhoea and constipation.

This crystal layout creates:
+ Nurturing
+ Emotional intelligence
+ Flexibility
+ Creativity
+ Healthy sexual relationships
+ Pleasure and passion

✦ Self-acceptance and gratitude
✦ Fulfilment of desires.

Crystals to use in this layout are:
✦ Two Carnelian
✦ Two Brown Tourmaline
✦ Two Rutilated Quartz
✦ Two Shiva Lingams
✦ Two Tiger's Eye.

Properties of the crystals:
✦ Carnelian: Enhances creativity
✦ Brown Tourmaline: Activates the base chakras and assists in healing sexual issues
✦ Rutilated Quartz: Assists in healing issues related to family handed down through the DNA
✦ Shiva Lingam: Severs all sexual cords and attachments and activates fertility
✦ Tiger's Eye: Allows you to see clearly into situations so you can make positive decisions.

Solar plexus chakra crystal layout

This crystal layout assists in transforming issues of:
✦ Emotional trauma
✦ Stagnancy in your life
✦ Inability to follow your dreams and ambitions
✦ Fear and anxiety
✦ Self-betrayal
✦ Suppressed emotions
✦ Lack of self-esteem
✦ Shame and guilt
✦ Poor digestion
✦ Over-controlling

+ Chronic fatigue
+ Disorders of the stomach, pancreas, gall bladder and liver.

This crystal layout creates:
+ Confidence
+ Freedom
+ Emotional balance
+ Appropriate self-discipline
+ Personal power and empowerment
+ Inner strength and courage
+ Determination.

Crystals to use in this layout are:
+ Two Mookite
+ Two Sodalite
+ Two Sunstone
+ Two Chrysocollas
+ Two Golden Calcite
+ Two Citrine.

Properties of the crystals:
+ Mookite: Assists in realising deep emotions such as sadness, fear and anger
+ Sodalite: Assists in healing issues of self-esteem and self-worth
+ Sunstone: Aligns your inner strength and the courage of the universe, assisting you to step into their power
+ Chrysocolla: Invites suppressed emotions to come to the surface for healing and release, while feeling supported and nurtured in the process
+ Golden Calcite: Allows you to find the determination required to step into your personal power
+ Citrine: Creates deep knowing of your self and the ability to live with an expanded awareness.

Heart chakra crystal layout

This crystal layout assists in transforming issues of:

+ Insensitivity
+ Sadness
+ Being judgmental
+ Rejection and abandonment
+ Lack of love and compassion
+ Jealousy
+ Grief; death of a loved one
+ All wounds of the heart
+ Relationships with self and others
+ Disorders of the heart, lungs, thymus, breasts, arms, shortness of breath, circulation problems, asthma, immune system deficiency, pain in the chest.

This crystal layout creates:

+ Balance
+ Joy and happiness
+ Unconditional love
+ Giving and receiving
+ Gratitude
+ Forgiveness
+ Inner peace
+ Love of self and others
+ Self-acceptance
+ Compassion.

Crystals to use in this layout are:

+ Two Rose Quartz
+ Two Green Aventurine
+ One Kunzite
+ Two Rhodochrosites
+ Two Malachite.

Properties of the crystals:

+ Rose Quartz: Activates deep love and peace within the heart
+ Green Aventurine: Heals and soothes the emotions of pain held within the heart
+ Kunzite: Activates the wisdom of love in the deeper chambers of the heart
+ Rhodochrosite: Powerful crystal for self-healing and acceptance
+ Malachite: Activates healing energy on all levels and penetrates love deep into every single cell of the body.

Throat chakra crystal layout

This crystal layout assists in transforming issues of:

+ Fear of speaking
+ Lack of expression
+ Difficulty putting feelings into words
+ Poor rhythm
+ Shyness
+ Blocked creative imagination
+ Inability to listen
+ Disorders of the throat, ears, voice, neck and tightness of the jaw.

This crystal layout creates:

+ Communication of truth
+ Listening
+ Finding our voice
+ Self-expression
+ Creativity

Crystals to use in this layout are:

+ One Blue Lace Agate
+ One Aquamarine
+ One Blue Kyanite.

Properties of the crystals:

+ Blue Lace Agate: Promotes peaceful flow of expression and calmness
+ Aquamarine: Supports in connecting to emotions and expressing how you feel from the heart
+ Blue Kyanite: Assists in releasing and letting go of old, stale energy and opens you up to free-flowing expression.

Third eye chakra crystal layout

This crystal layout assists in transforming issues of:

+ Lack of imagination
+ Lack of visions and dreams
+ Mind chatter and scattered mind
+ Lack of spiritual vision
+ Lack of clarity and intuition
+ Subconscious blockages
+ Poor vision and memory
+ Denial and delusion
+ Headaches and physical sight.

This crystal layout creates:

+ Deeper intuition
+ Clarity
+ Clear vision
+ Expanded awareness
+ Calm mind
+ Visualisation
+ Dream recall
+ Good memory
+ Awakened imagination
+ Insight
+ Psychic development.

Crystals to use in this layout are:

+ One Azurite
+ One Amethyst
+ One Lapis Lazuli
+ One Fluorite.

Properties of the crystals:

+ Azurite: Expands our awareness to see old patterns and beliefs in a new light
+ Amethyst: Balances the right and left hemispheres of the brain, calming the mind and creating relaxation; overall healing crystal that opens you to psychic abilities
+ Lapis Lazuli: Stimulates and deepens spiritual awareness
+ Fluorite: Balances the mind and mental body.

Crown chakra crystal layout

This crystal layout assists in transforming issues of:

+ Spiritual trauma
+ Confusion
+ Disconnection from source and self
+ Lack of wisdom and knowledge
+ Feeling of not belonging
+ Distorted beliefs
+ Lack of love and joy
+ Lack of direction.

This crystal layout creates:

+ Union with higher self and source
+ Divine wisdom and knowledge
+ Clarity
+ Bliss
+ Oneness and wholeness
+ Enhancement of your ability to learn

+ Lightness of being
+ Spiritual awareness.

Crystals to use in this layout are:
+ One Clear Quartz
+ One Angelite
+ One Selenite.

Properties of the crystals:
+ Quartz: Amplifies and deepens the love and wisdom from the universe
+ Angelite: Aligns us to the higher realms of existence to connect to and receive wisdom and guidance
+ Selenite: Opens the crown chakra and brings in high-vibration light and love down through the chakras into the physical plane, connecting you to your higher self.

STAR CRYSTAL GRIDS FOR HEALING AND MANIFESTATION

Star grids are another way to use the powerful medicine of the crystals and the energy that is created when working with the six-pointed star grid formation. This time we are working with two different crystal energies and Devas, and laying the crystals in the six-pointed star grid around the body. The six-pointed star is a powerful ally in grounding and amplifying the healing medicine of the crystals, especially when placed in this grid format.

The Crystal Kingdom has guided me to create the following various types of sacred star grids, to assist in connecting and grounding individual types of energies in the body, mind and spirit. These bring about the activation of the healing energy that is already within, promoting deep healing and manifesting this into your physical reality, depending on the energy of the grid and what your soul is calling for at the time.

The star grids are a very potent and powerful healing process, creating tangible positive shifts in your life. They are a great tool and support on your journey, deepening your understanding of yourself, healing and the Crystal Kingdom.

Choose a grid that aligns with the type of healing you are looking for and follow the activation process at the end of this chapter to guide you step-by-step on how to work with the grids. Each specific sacred star grid will select different crystals; however, the layout and activation are the same. Each star grid has two specific crystal medicines and you require 15 of each of the crystals to be laid on and around the body on certain points (it is preferable to work with tumble stones). If finding 15 of each crystal is a challenge, you can work with six crystals, placing them only on the six points around the body. You can also make a crystal essence of your two chosen crystals in the grid and place a drop of the essence and crystal energy on each point.

The star grid is laid on and around the body while you lie on the floor or a flat comfortable surface. You can work with these grids on yourself or facilitate the healing on someone else. If you are doing the healing on yourself, at first it is a good idea to have someone with you to assist in placing the crystals on the specific points. Once the grid is created, relax into the sacred space and breathe the crystal energy in and out of your heart for eight minutes, filling every cell of your being with this crystal medicine. After the eight minutes your body, mind and spirit will be resonating with the energy of the grid. The energy will be flowing out into your aura and you will be completely immersed in this vibration.

The following star grids will help connect and ground energies in the body, mind and spirit. This will activate the healing energy that is already within, promoting deep healing.

Inner child grid allows for childhood memories to come to the surface for understanding and healing, opening the heart and bringing back the innocence, joy and freedom of our spirit.
+ Aventurine: Connects to and heals deep wounds and patterns from your childhood.

+ Rose Quartz: Opens the heart as it brings unconditional love to the emotions and draws the energy inwards as it activates the wisdom of the heart.

Expanded heart grid assists in healing old wounds of the heart, allowing us to feel free and safe to love unconditionally.
+ Rose Quartz: Opens the heart and nurtures the soul.
+ Golden Calcite: Brings in the loving light of the universe.

Grounding and purification grid assists in grounding your energy into the Earth, allowing you to feel safe, supported, nurtured and protected. This powerful cleansing and purifying grid also allows more clarity and focus in your life.
+ Hematite: Grounds and connects to the centre of the Earth, enhancing manifestation skills.
+ Black Tourmaline: Powerful grounding and protective crystal.

Emotional healing grid brings balance and understanding to old suppressed emotions for transmutation and transformation, making way for more feelings of love and joy.
+ Chrysocolla: Brings old emotions to the surface for transmutation in a gentle, supporting way.
+ Rhodochrosite: Creates emotional intelligence and assists in dissolving fears.

Physical healing grid creates deep healing on the physical plane, assisting the body to heal itself. Great to use when there are any issues or disease within the physical body.
+ Malachite: Deep physical healing crystal that also penetrates into all levels and promotes overall healing.
+ Bloodstone: Allows you to connect to the innate healing energy of the physical body, supporting it to heal itself.

Life purpose grid opens you to the awareness of your life purposes and manifests it in your life with ease and grace, allowing you the strength and courage to walk your path.

- Sugilite: Strengthens your ability to walk your life purpose and life path.
- Amazonite: Aligns you to your life purpose and encourages you to step onto your path with strength and courage.

Goddess grid connects you to the goddess energy that lives within us all and assists in healing any wounds connected to our feminine power.
- Chrysocolla: Connection to the sacred goddess within.
- Larimar: Awakens the goddess within, allowing for deep healing of our feminine.

Self-empowerment grid enhances your strength and courage to stand strong in your essence and power in a deep place of love.
- Sunstone: Awakens self-empowerment, creating strength and courage.
- Golden Calcite: Enhances personal power in your life.

Kundalini activation grid assists in activating and integrating the Kundalini and life-force energy, allowing for an awakening and deepening of your creative flow, and enhancing your spark and inspiration for life. The Kundalini energy is held within the base of the spine and when activated a profound spiritual awakening can occur.
- Serpentine: Stimulates the Kundalini energy to be released within the body.
- Jet: Activates the Kundalini energy and creative spark within the body.

Soul retrieval grid assists in the process of soul retrieval, connecting to the lost aspect of ourselves that has been left in a time and space due to some form of shock or trauma. This grid draws back the positive aspects so you can feel more at peace with yourself.

✦ Sharman Stone: Assists and facilitates soul retrieval journeys.

✦ Galena: Promotes and supports soul retrieval journeys.

Astral travel grid supports and enhances experiences of astral travelling.

✦ Moldavite: Supports astral travelling into different times, places and dimensions.

✦ Stibnite: Enhances and supports the astral travel journey.

Divine magic grid assists you to connect to the magic and wonder of life, the Earth, the universe and yourself.

✦ Labradorite: Assists in awakening the magic of your soul.

✦ Cinnabar: Invites the energy of joy and magic in your life on all levels.

Self-expression grid assists you to find your voice and speak your truth from a place of love.

✦ Turquoise: Assists in communication of truth from the heart.

✦ Aquamarine: Helps you to connect to and express your own wisdom and knowledge.

Earth healing grid grounds high vibrational energy into the Earth to assist in her healing and awakening.

✦ Garnet: Connects to and draws up the healing energy of the Earth.

✦ Smoky Quartz: Enhances a deep connection to Mother Earth and her healing vibration.

Sacred divine partner grid assists in manifesting, attracting or deepening a sacred divine union with another.

✦ Pink Kunzite: Opens and aligns the heart chakra to Divine Love.

✦ Morganite: Releases self-sabotaging and old relationship patterns, allowing a new way of loving unconditionally.

Creative grid assists in connecting to and awakening your creative abilities, and to amplifying your passions and talents, allowing a powerful creative energy to flow so you feel inspired in your life.

+ Carnelian: Enhances and awakens creativity within the soul.
+ Fire Agate: Deepens your passion and spark for life, fuelling your internal flame.

Relaxation grid creates a sacred space to delve deeply into relaxation as it supports and nurtures you to let go of mind chatter, promoting relaxation of the mind, body and soul.

+ Golden Calcite: Promotes deep relaxation and calms the mind.
+ Amethyst: Balances the left and right hemispheres of the brain, allowing you to enter into deep meditation and relaxation.

Abundance grid supports you to create, open and receive abundance in all aspects of your life.

+ Citrine: Assists in manifesting wealth and abundance.
+ Jade: Creates abundance and good fortune.

Spirituality grid enhances your connection to the cosmos, deepening and opening your awareness to deep spiritual knowing and wisdom.

+ Danburite: Enhances your spirituality, psychic development and channelling abilities.
+ Pietersite: Supports your spiritual awakening.

Angel grid assists in connecting to the Angelic Realm to receive their divine blessings, guidance and healing.

+ Angelite: Aligns us to the Angelic Realm where we receive healing and divine guidance.
+ Celestite: Connects and communicates with the Angelic Realm.

Fairy grid connects you with the nature sprits of the Earth and the fairy kingdom to create magic and healing, reminding you to play, laugh and have joy in your life.

+ Amber: Allows a deep connection to the nature and tree sprits.
+ Spirit Quartz: Connects to the fairy realm and nature spirits, creating a sense of magic in your life.

Embracing the shadow grid invites you to accept the unloved traits of yourself that play out in your life, bringing them into the light and awareness as you learn how to love all aspects of yourself in your totality, setting yourself free.

+ Black Tourmaline: Transmutes and dissolves any stuck or dormant energies in the body and auric field, creating a deep and powerful cleansing and purification.
+ Black Obsidian: Allows old habits and traits to surface so you can love and accept all of your self in its totality. Allows you to enter into the void to receive wisdom and knowledge from your shadow side.

Releasing karmic patterns (past life) grid brings awareness to old patterns that play out in your life, so you understand where the patterns started, realise the gift from the experience, and let go of the patterns with love and gratitude.

+ Lapis Lazuli: Supports past life awareness and heals any karmic patterns.
+ Apophyllite: Assists in releasing old karmic patterns.

Ancestral karmic patterns grid understands and dissolves the patterns handed down from your family, allowing you to receive the love and wisdom from this experience and create a new way of being for yourself and your future ancestors, completing the cycle.

+ Amber: Assists in dissolving old patterns from the past that are handed down through the DNA and family.
+ Petrified Wood: Connects to our ancestors and their healing wisdom.

Star grid layout and activation

Choose your star grid from the previous pages, then use the following example to lay the grid out and activate the crystal energy.

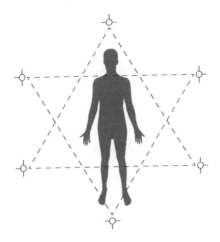

You will need 15 of each crystal from your chosen star grid.

+ Place one of each crystal on the seven chakra points:
+ Place one of each crystal in each hand
+ Place one of each crystal on the star points shown in the above grid

Follow these steps to activate your star grid.

+ Play soothing, relaxing music. Set your sacred space by lighting a candle and clear the space of any unwanted energies by burning sage or simply by setting an intention.
+ Set your intention for the healing. What would you like to receive from this healing space? Your intention will usually be the same as the intention of the grid you have chosen.
+ Lie down in a comfortable position and place crystals on the allocated points.
+ Call and invoke the Devas of the crystals you are working with. Ask them to shower upon you the healing medicine of their essence as they bathe you in their love.
+ As you inhale, breathe down the golden light of the universe through your crown chakra into your physical body. Breathe this light into every cell of your being, then send it down and out the bottom of your feet, anchoring it into the Earth.

✦ Now breathe the healing energy of the Earth up through your feet and into your heart.

✦ Allow this energy of the Earth and the energy of the cosmos to enter deeply into your heart as you become a conduit for the light moving down from the cosmos and the love moving up from the Earth.

✦ Now bring your attention to the crystals that lay around and upon you.

✦ Feel the energy of the crystals amplify and expand as you become aware of their presence.

✦ Breathe in the crystal energy and potent crystal medicine into your heart.

✦ Feel your heart expand as it receives the love of the crystals.

✦ Now send this crystal energy and medicine to every cell of your being.

✦ Keep breathing the love of the crystals into your heart and into every cell.

✦ Every now and then breathe the crystal energy out to your aura.

✦ Continue breathing deeply, amplifying the crystal energy with every breath you take.

✦ Keep breathing this way for eight minutes.

✦ Bring your attention and awareness into the room and slowly open your eyes.

Similarly to the healing process of the chakra balancing, it will take a few days to integrate the healing of the star grid. Thoughts, feelings and emotions could arise as you let go of the old and allow the new to create healing in your life. Follow the same nurturing suggestions mentioned previously for crystal chakra healing

The following crystals all hold powerful and transformational healing properties. Some crystals definitely have more than one healing medicine and some crystals hold similar energies. This is a quick and easy reference guide to assist you in finding the crystals that best suit your intention for healing.

CRYSTALS FOR HEALING

Abandonment	Diopside, Red Jasper, Kunzite
Abundance	Chrysanthemum Stone, Citrine, Jade, Peridot
Abuse	Larimar, Malachite, Ruby
Acceptance	Rhodocrosite, Awakening Crystal, Rose Quartz
Acne	Agate, Jade, Malachite
Addictive behaviours	Amethyst, Green Apatite, Hiddenite, Awakening Crystal
AIDS	Cuprite, Hematite, Bloodstone
Akashic Records	Pietersite
Alcoholism	Amethyst, Awakening Crystal
Amplification	Clear Quartz
Ancestors	Amber, Red Jasper, Petrified Wood, Shaman Stone
Ancient wisdom	Red Jasper, Lapis Lazuli, Serpentine, Ancient Wisdom Crystal
Angelic Realm	Angelite, Celestite, Danburite, Seraphinite
Anger	Carnelian, Diamond, Dioptase, Mookite, Ocean Jasper, Larimar, Brown Tourmaline
Anxiety	Amethyst, Ruby, Rutilated Quartz, Smoky Quartz, Stibnite, Apache Tears
Appendix	Emerald, Malachite
Appropriate boundaries	Black Tourmaline, Emerald

Arthritis	Rhodonite, Obsidian, Opal
Artistic gifts	Fire Agate
Ascended masters	Danburite
Assertiveness	Lapis Lazuli, Chrysoprase
Asthma	Pink or Green Tourmaline, Chrysocolla
Astral travel	Stibnite
Back	Malachite, Chrysocolla
Balance	Boji Stones™, Chrysanthemum Stone, Hematite, Red Jasper, Spirit Quartz, Garnet
Beauty	Peridot, Moonstone
Birthing	Opal, Moonstone, Rose Quartz, Larimar
Bladder	Bloodstone, Jasper
Blood disorders	Carnelian, Bloodstone, Hematite, Malachite, Galena
Blood pressure	Cuprite, Hematite
Bones	Calcite, Malachite
Brain	Amethyst, Ametrine, Natrolite, Pyrite
Breasts	Rose Quartz, Green Tourmaline
Breathing	Rhodochrosite, Cuprite, Smoky Quartz
Broken bones	Tiger's Eye, Hematite, Calcite
Broken heart	Pink or Green Tourmaline, Rose Quartz
Calm	Blue Lace Agate, Golden Calcite, Sodalite
Cancer	Cuprite, Sugilite
Cardiovascular	Angelite
Cartilage	Amber, Apatite
Ceremonies	Bustamite, Opal, Red Jasper, Phenacite
Change	Apache Tears, Hematite, Black Obsidian, Sunstone, Brown Tourmaline

Channelling	Cacoxenite, Danburite, Divine Temple
Circulation	Hematite, Tiger Iron, Jasper, Garnet
Clairvoyance	Lapis Lazuli, Amethyst, Azurite
Clarity	Tanzanite, Pietersite, Clear Quartz, Seraphinite, Topaz
Clear communication	Blue Lace Agate, Aquamarine, Chrysocolla
Clear vision	Azurite, Blue Apatite
Co-dependency	Carnelian
Colds	Malachite, Kunzite, Citrine
Comfort eating	Hiddenite
Commitment	Diamond, Garnet, Orpiment, Peridot
Compassion	Green Aventurine, Emerald, Rhodochrosite, Rose Quartz, Watermelon Tourmaline
Concentration	Pyrite, Fluorite, Amethyst
Conception	Garnet, Carnelian, Moonstone
Confidence	Chrysoberyl, Helidor
Confusion	Pyrite, Lapis Lazuli, Fluorite, Aquamarine
Coughs	Agate, Malachite, Kunzite
Courage	Amazonite, Carnelian, Galena, Tiger's Eye, Sunstone
Creation of gifts	Cacoxenite, Carnelian, Spirit Quartz
Creative blocks	Fire Agate, Carnelian, Red Tourmaline
Creative ideas	Brazilianite, Cacoxenite
Creativity	Fire Agate, Red Tourmaline, Carnelian, Ruby, Moonstone
Dark night of the soul	Black Obsidian
Decision making	Brazilianite, Fluorite, Tiger's Eye
Dehydration	Agate, Blue Lace Agate, Aquamarine

Depression	Sunstone, Larimar, Awakening Crystal
Detoxifying	Hematite, Selenite, Black Tourmaline
Diabetes	Blue Lace Agate, Citrine
Digestion	Agate, Jasper, Topaz
Direction	Moonstone, Seraphinite, Tektite
Disease	Amber, Malachite
Dissolving fears	Rhodochrosite, Smoky Quartz, Black Tourmaline
Divine guidance	Angelite, Phenacite, Danburite
Divine masculine	Shiva Lingam, Sunstone
Divine source	Celestite, Sunstone
Divine union	Bixbite, Diamond
DNA	Amber, Rutilated Quartz
Dog bite	Hematite, Black Tourmaline
Dreams	Amethyst, Moldavite, Herkimer Diamond
Ears	Obsidian, Amethyst
Earth	Chiastolite, Cuprite, Hematite, Red Jasper, Green Tourmaline, Shaman Stone
Emotions	Awakening Crystal, Aquamarine, Green Aventurine, Rose Quartz, Malachite, Larimar
Empowerment	Larimar, Sunstone, Helidor
Endometriosis	Chrysoprase, Chrysocolla
Endurance	Nuummite
Energy, increasing	Selenite, Quartz
Entity removal	Nuummite, Black Tourmaline, Shaman Stone
Epilepsy	Kunzite, Sugilite
Exhaustion	Ruby, Quartz, Turquoise

Expression	Blue Lace Agate, Aquamarine, Blue Kyanite
Eyesight	Malachite, Aquamarine, Blue Lace Agate, Labradorite
Faith	Goethite, Kunzite
Fallopian tubes	Moonstone, Chrysocolla
Family	Amber, Apophyllite, Zincite
Fear	Apache Tears, Diopside, Ruby, Truth Crystal, Black Tourmaline
Feet	Smoky Quartz
Feminine	Ajoite, Aquamarine, Chrysocolla, Cuprite, Larimar, Moonstone, Goddess Crystal
Fertility	Moonstone, Shiva Lingam
Fibromyalgia	Aventurine, Topaz
Fiery temper	Blue Lace Agate, Ruby
Flexibility	Brazilianite, Heliodor
Focus	Fluorite, Lapis Lazuli, Pyrite, Amethyst
Forgiveness	Pink Tourmaline, Green Tourmaline, Watermelon Tourmaline
Gall bladder	Calcite, Obsidian, Amber
Glands	Agate, Tourmaline
Goddess	Ajoite, Chrysoberyl, Larimar
Grace	Pink Tourmaline
Gratitude	Hiddenite, Peridot
Grief	Apache Tears, Goethite, Ruby, Black Tourmaline
Grounding	Hematite, Apache Tears, Mookite, Petrified Wood
Guilt	Pink Tourmaline, Rose Quartz

Habits	Amethyst, Awakening Crystal
Hair	Jade, Petrified Wood
Hands	Smoky Quartz
Harmony	Chrysanthemum Stone, Jade
Headaches	Jet, Amethyst, Obsidian
Healthy boundaries	Red Japer, Stibnite
Hearing	Rose Quartz, Kunzite, Dioptase
Heart	Tourmaline, Kunzite, Rose Quartz, Dioptase
Higher realms	Danburite, Phenacite, Shattuckite
Higher self	Dumortierite, Selenite, Topaz
Honesty	Turquoise
Hope	Garnet, Dioptase
Hormones	Aquamarine, Garnet
Hospitalisation	Hematite, Black Tourmaline
Illumination	Scolecite
Imagination	Cacoxenite, Tanzanite
Immune system	Mookite, Agate, Calcite, Malachite
Impotency	Ruby, Garnet, Carnelian
Infection	Malachite, Blue Lace Agate
Inner child	Green Aventurine, Diopside, Rose Quartz
Inner peace	Brazilianite, Danburite, Rose Quartz
Inner truths	Tiger's Eye
Insect bites	Blue Lace Agate, Malachite
Insight	Labradorite, Fluorite, Azurite, Lapis Lazuli, Tiger's Eye
Insomnia	Sodalite, Hematite, Amethyst
Inspiration	Fire Agate, Herkimer Diamond, Spirit Quartz, Emerald, Amethyst

Integrity	Turquoise
Intelligence	Pyrite, Fluorite
Intimacy	Diamond, Emerald, Moonstone
Intuition	Azurite, Purpurite, Lapis Lazuli
Itching	Blue Lace Agate, Blue Tourmaline
Jealousy	Chrysoprase, Rhodonite
Joints	Rhodonite, Malachite
Joy	Citrine, Opal, Spirit Quartz
Karmic patterns	Apophyllite, Lapis Lazuli
Kidneys	Opal, Amber, Hematite
Knowledge	Lapis Lazuli, Divine Truth Crystal
Kundalini	Crocoite, Fulgurite, Jet, Serpentine
Leadership	Heliodor, Sunstone
Learning	Fluorite
Letting go	Blue Kyanite, Blue Tourmaline
Legs	Black Kyanite, Smoky Quartz
Lethargy	Fire Opal, Quartz
Life purpose	Seraphinite, Sugilite, Amazonite
Light beings	Libyan Gold Tektite, Moldavite, Tektite
Liver	Mookite, Bloodstone, Malachite
Loss	Goddess Crystal, Awakening Crystal, Morganite
Love	Morganite, Dioptase, Diamond, Kunzite
Lungs	Hiddenite, Emerald
Lupus	Aragonite, Mookite
Lymph	Blue Lace Agate, Malachite
Magic	Labrodrite, Spirit Quartz
Magnificence	Herkimer Diamond, Rhodonite

Manifestation	Hematite, Libyan Gold Tektite, Pyrite
Meditation	Amethyst, Calcite, Nirvana Quartz, Rhodonite
Memory	Fluorite, Pyrite, Ametrine
Menopause	Chrysoprase, Aquamarine, Moonstone
Menstrual issues	Chrysoprase, Moonstone, Bloodstone
Migraines	Amethyst, Dioptase
Money issues	Citrine, Jade
Mother Earth	Agate, Diopside, Red Jasper, Smoky Quartz, Hematite, Goethite
Mother issues (healing)	Diopside
Motivation	Selenite, Helidor, Clear Quartz
Mouth	Celestite, Flourite
Moving forward	Selenite, Chyrosocolla
Muscles	Celestite, Calcite, Malachite
Music	Spirit Quartz
Nails (fingers and toes)	Agate, Calcite
Nature spirits	Peridot, Spirit Quartz, Green Tourmaline
Nervous system	Galena, Green Tourmaline, Awakening Crystal
New beginnings	Selenite, Moonstone
New ideas	Herkimer Diamond, Blue Kyanite
New projects	Moonstone, Orpiment
Nightmares	Amethyst, Herkimer Diamond
Obesity	Petrified Wood
Ovaries	Moonstone
Pain	Malachite
Pancreas	Carnelian, Blue Lace Agate
Passion	Fire Agate, Bixbite, Ruby, Eudialyte
Past life	Apophyllite, Lapis Lazuli

Patience	Pyromorphite, Rose Quartz
Peace	Golden Calcite, Danburite, Celestite
Performance anxiety	Hematite, Sugilite
Personal power	Garnet, Rhodonite, Sunstone
Physical	Bloodstone, Malachite
Physical wounds	Malachite, Aventurine
Pineal	Citrine, Calcite, Labradorite
Pituitary	Labradorite, Danburite
Play	Cinnabar
Power animal	Boji Stones™, Chrysotile
Pregnancy	Pearl, Moonstone, Shiva Lingam
Present in the moment	Brookite, Fluorite, Sugilite
Prosperity	Citrine, Quartz, Jade
Prostate	Serpentine, Opal
Protection	Shungite, Black Tourmaline
Psychic abilities	Amethyst, Charoite, Lapis Lazuli
Purification	Hematite, Selenite, Black Tourmaline
Rash	Bloodstone, Calcite, Malachite
Rebirth	Sunstone, Shiva Lingam, Moonstone
Reflection	Amazonite, Cuprite, Rhodonite, Reflection Crystal
Rejection	Diopside, Kunzite
Relationship	Morganite, Prehnite, Diamond
Relaxation	Calcite, Blue Lace Agate, Amethyst
Resentment	Ocean Jasper, Kunzite
Responsibility	Heliodor, Sunstone
Rites of passage	Bustamite, Cuprite
Sadness	Dioptase, Malachite, Brown Tourmaline
Self-acceptance	Nirvana Stone, Rhodochrosite, Rose Quartz, Sodalite, Eudialyte

Self-awareness	Brazilianite, Blue Kyanite
Self-betrayal	Kunzite
Self-confidence	Fire Agate, Sodalite
Self-discipline	Chrysoprase
Self-empowerment	Sunstone, Brazilianite, Charoite, Heliodor
Self-esteem	Pyromorphite, Sodalite, Chrysoprase, Rose Quartz, Rhodochrosite
Self-mastery	Nuummite, Chrysoberyl
Self-nurture	Chrysoprase, Diopside, Nirvana Quartz, Prehnite, Rose Quartz
Self-worth	Sodalite, Nirvana Quartz
Sensitivity	Green Aventurine, Larimar
Sensuality	Diamond, Garnet
Serenity	Lepidolite, Tibetan Quartz
Sexuality	Crocoite
Shadow self	Cuprite, Nuummite, Black Tourmaline, Black Obsidian, Reflection Crystal
Shaman	Nuummite, Shaman Stone
Shamanic journeying	Agate, Shaman Stone
Shock	Bloodstone, Hematite
Skeletal system	Calcite
Skin	Rose Quartz, Agate
Smoking (stop)	Awakening Crystal, Hematite
Sorrow	Sugilite, Amazonite, Awakening Crystal
Soul retrieval	Boji Stones™, Galena, Shaman Stone
Spirit animal	Agate, Chrysotile
Spiritual awakening	Pietersite, Danburite, Amethyst
Stagnant energy	Spirit Quartz, Black Tourmaline

Staying focused	Tiger's Eye
Stillness	Cuprite, Nirvana Quartz
Stress	Amethyst, Calcite
Success	Orpiment, Vivianite
Tantric union	Crocoite, Diamond, Bixbite
Teacher	Shattuckite
Teeth	Fluorite, Aquamarine
Throat	Turquoise, Blue Kyanite, Aquamarine
Thymus	Peridot, Aquamarine
Thyroid	Blue Lace Agate, Chrysocolla
Tongue	Sodalite
Tranquillity	Calcite, Celestite, Nirvana Quartz, Scolecite
Trauma	Chrysocolla, Diopside, Hematite, Awakening Crystal, Ruby
Tree Devas	Amber, Agate, Petrified Wood
Trust	Azurite, Garnet, Libyan Gold Tektite, Cinnabar
Truth	Charoite, Chrysoberyl, Lepidolite, Divine Truth
Tumours	Malachite, Dioptase
Veins	Cuprite, Obsidian
Vision	Azurite, Lapis Lazuli
Vision quests	Opal, Shaman Stone
Visionary stone	Purpurite, Blue Apatite
Voice	Aquamarine, Blue Kyanite
Vulnerability	Ajoite, Diamond
Weight, losing	Green Apatite
Wellbeing	Azurite, Calcite
Worry	Amethyst, Moonstone, Fluorite

DISTANCE HEALING WITH CRYSTALS

Having a loving thought about someone is a form of distant healing. By setting an intention to send someone love and healing, it is done. Healing does not have to be local to work; the person you are doing healing with does not have to be in the same room. This has been proven scientifically. When we have a thought it travels around the universe and back to us at the speed of light. The same process happens with distant healing. When working with the power of intention to send the healing energy to someone or something, the intention acts like a funnel, allowing the energy to travel through space and time to reach the person you intended your intention to flow to.

Crystals have the ability to amplify energies. When working with the crystals in distance healing, the crystal will assist in amplifying the healing energy of love. When you send healing to another, it is very important to see them as already healed. See this divine soul as perfect, whole and complete as you express this to the universe with certainty.

Sending healing energy

To send healing energy, follow these steps.

- ✦ Choose a pointed crystal, preferably double terminated quartz.
- ✦ Guide yourself into a relaxed and centred space.
- ✦ Call upon the Deva of the crystal, your Guides and Healing Angels for their love and support.
- ✦ Open and allow yourself to become a channel or conduit for universal healing energy.
- ✦ Say the following healing invocation three times:

> *I invoke the love of the divine universe within my heart*
> *I am a clear and pure channel*
> *Love is my guide*

+ Close your eyes and start to focus on your breath.
+ Call upon the light and love of the universe, and start to breathe and draw this into your crown chakra.
+ Allow this healing light and love to fill every single cell of your being.
+ Bring your attention to your heart space, filling yourself with love.
+ Visualise and feel yourself shining and radiating pure love from your heart, feeling at peace and full of serenity.
+ Bring your crystal to your heart, and send love and compassion into the crystal.
+ Now visualise the person you would like to send the love to.
+ Working with the crystal, send and offer the love from deep within your heart, the love of the universe and the love of the Earth to this person.
+ See them receiving this love and see them as perfect, whole and complete, radiating, full of light. Ask that every cell in their being be brought back to perfect harmony with their higher self as you visualise their whole body full of healing energy.
+ Do this for as long as it feels appropriate; you will intuitively know when to stop.
+ To finish the healing, visualise the person in a golden sphere of light and see them merge into it. Thank your Guides and Angels.

TEACHER CRYSTALS (MASTER CRYSTALS)

There is a unique group of powerful crystals within the Crystal Kingdom called Teacher Crystals, or Masters as they are most commonly known. These powerful crystals are recognised by their many and various geometrical shapes and sizes that create potent energies to assist us in awakening our full potential. The many different shapes, Angels and pure forms that these crystals manifest create and hold specific vibrations. These crystals hold the secrets to awakening your inner teacher and the master within.

By working with and connecting to these Teacher Crystals of pure structure and vibration we start to understand ourselves and the magic of the universe. As we continue to delve deep within our own soul to discover the love and wisdom within, we truly start to follow the guidance of our own loving hearts.

Teacher Crystals mirror, amplify and ignite the master within. They are most commonly found in Clear Quartz, Smoky Quartz and Citrine. Some of these beautiful crystals have been polished, but they are not artificially shaped as this is how they are formed naturally, deep within the Earth.

My understanding is that most of the Master Crystals were discovered and named by Katrina Raphaell, a knowledgeable and respected crystal healer. Katrina spent time studying Sacred Geometry and how it relates to the Crystal Kingdom. I would like to take this opportunity to acknowledge and honour Katrina for all the wisdom she has shared from the Crystal Kingdom. Katrina is my teacher's teacher and a lot of her healing processes have allowed me to open, deepen and awaken to my own healing and wisdom from my own unique and potent experiences.

Katrina named and categorised the Master Crystals; however, I have changed their name to Teacher Crystals and renamed each individual crystal due to my own experience. I would now love to share with you my own understanding and connection with them, which are at times similar to Katrina's.

Over the years I have worked closely with the Teacher Crystals and my experiences with these energies have touched me deeply with lessons of love and transformation, assisting me to connect to the master within. These crystals can be purchased readily at crystal shops. When you are ready to connect to such a vibration, these crystals find their way to you.

Please now let me share with you some of my favourite Teacher Crystals and how to identify them. I invite you to open and awaken to their powerful healing vibration.

Divine Temple Crystal (Cathedral Lightbrary Crystal)

The Divine Temple Crystal (Cathedral Lightbrary Crystal) Is one of the most powerful crystals on Earth. To identify this sacred piece look for a crystal that is quite large and has many crystal points around the main body making their way up to a larger point at the top. These amazing beings of light are here to assist you to connect, attune and align to the Akashic Records, a place held within the universe where every thought, feeling and experience from every lifetime is recorded and stored. This powerful crystal is called a divine temple, because it is a place to enter and connect with the divine source of the universe. When you sit in union with this powerful crystal the gates of Heaven open and you connect to all that is. This divine temple of light is a sacred place to receive renewal, meditation and healing, and to access universal wisdom. This crystal has been used in group connection as a council of light. Each person of the group enters into a different chamber of the crystal, receiving divine guidance and direction.

This crystal assists in:

+ connecting to the Akashic Records
+ connecting to the love and wisdom of the universe
+ group bonding and connection
+ reaching deep states of meditation
+ uplifting group consciousness
+ accessing universal knowledge
+ becoming a pure channel of energy.

Goddess Crystal (Isis Crystal)

To identify a Goddess Crystal look for a crystal that has a main face consisting of five edges. These five edges are aligned in perfect geometry. The first edge is at the base of the face, two smaller edges of the same length extend up from the bottom edge and two longer edges extend from the smaller edges to reach a point at the top of the face. If the two smaller edges that extend from the base are longer than the edges that extend to create the point at the top, it creates a whole new geometry and the crystal is not classed as an Isis.

The Goddess Crystal holds within it the secrets of the divine feminine. This amazing crystal aligns with the goddesses of compassion, especially the goddess Isis. The story of Isis shares with us the inner strength and courage she bestowed when her beloved was killed and taken from her. She had to sit with her pain of grief, separation, betrayal and loss. After much inner work, Isis finally found a place of forgiveness and surrender within her heart. Once she reached this place within, her beloved was brought back to her.

This story highlights the deep powerful energy the Goddess Crystal holds. It assists us to look within, sit with our painful emotions and from this sacred place transform to a place of deep inner healing. This crystal assists you to drop deep into your heart, showing the ways to self-love, self-healing, nurturing and compassion. Being such a powerful crystal of feminine energy, the Goddess Crystal also assists in balancing the masculine and feminine, allowing for the opportunity to heal that comes from this sacred union, where you feel safe to open completely to pure vulnerability, as true love and healing is received.

The Goddess Crystal also aligns with Mother Mary and the Goddess Quan Yin, holding powerful healing energy of these compassionate masters. The crystal is a must for those on the healing journey because it resonates with the wisdom and knowledge of the secrets to healing. The Goddess Crystal will also assist in your connection with our Divine Mother Earth, sharing this powerful nurturing space as you connect to her divine feminine.

This crystal assists in:

- ✦ discovering compassion and unconditional love
- ✦ experiencing powerful self-love and healing
- ✦ finding inner strength and courage
- ✦ becoming empowered

+ overcoming deep emotions of betrayal and grief
+ deep healing of the emotional body
+ discovering the secrets of healing
+ deeply connecting to Mother Earth
+ awakening the divine feminine
+ balancing the masculine and feminine.

Truth Crystal (Channelling Crystal)

A Truth Crystal has seven edges that make up the main face and a triangle on the opposite side. These edges can consist of different lengths, as long as seven edges make up the main face.

The geometry of seven creates the energy of those special souls that embark on the life-long journey of awakening their truth. The triangle at the back of the crystal allows for this truth to manifest into the physical form and into your life. This amazing crystal allows you to look deep within your soul, where we find our own divine wisdom and personal truth, supporting and assisting in creating this truth in your life and in stepping fully onto the path of self-empowerment. It connects us to the love and wisdom of the universe where all truth is held, allowing us to align with the highest truth of all. As we connect and align with this high vibrational light, we become a pure beacon of love and wisdom. The Truth Crystal is a wonderful friend for anyone who works as a medium, tarot reader, automatic writer or angel intuit. Having this crystal present assists in bringing through the wisdom and information you are seeking and allowing you to open and receive this wisdom with a deep knowing, creating true realisation.

This crystal assists in:
+ experiencing self-empowerment
+ discovering personal truth
+ connecting to and channelling the wisdom of the cosmos
+ connecting to your internal knowledge
+ obtaining love and wisdom from within your soul.

Divine Truth Crystal
(Channelling Dow Crystal)

The Divine Truth Crystal has a very similar geometry
to the Channelling Crystal. It has seven edges and
three triangles. The Divine Truth Crystal has the
same structure as the Truth Crystal repeated three times. When we
connect to the energy of this powerful master we are working with the
pure energy of Christ consciousness. It holds the same properties as the
Truth Crystal; however, it works on a higher vibration and is a great
crystal for personal healing and awakening.

This crystal assists in:

+ connecting to Christ consciousness
+ dissolving past life patterns
+ creating harmony in your life
+ manifesting your dreams and goals
+ connecting to the magnificence of All That Is
+ increasing intuitive awareness
+ meditating
+ creating balance.

Awakening Crystal (Elestial Crystal)

Identifying an Awakening Crystal can be a
little tricky at first; however, once you get to
know them you certainly don't miss them.
Awakening Crystals are mostly formed in
Smoky Quartz and look like a group of crystal points laid over the top of
each other.

It is said that these sacred crystals are gifts from the Angelic Realm.
Sharing from my own personal experience, the Elestial Crystal is
one of the most powerful crystals on the Earth and a true gift to our
planet at this time of transformation. It holds within it the secrets to
healing the emotional body on a massive scale, working with group

consciousness and assisting the planet in bringing oneness to our world community. Connecting to an Awakening Crystal allows us to receive clarity on our emotional wounds, gaining a sense of emotional intelligence and wellbeing. It amplifies buried emotions, allowing them to surface while supporting and holding us as we delve deep into the wound. As our heart opens and self-love is experienced, our awareness expands to receive the gift from such a challenge. Once these emotions are brought into balance, you feel less addiction, depression, anxiety and separation in your life.

The Awakening Crystal is great for those who have embarked on the journey of loving and accepting the shadow side of their psyche because it holds a safe, powerful space to look deep within your hidden chambers. It also assists in creating awareness around why and how people trigger us. We would not see something in someone else unless we had it within ourselves. Taking this understanding into consideration, if someone 'pushes your buttons' or triggers something emotionally within you, then they are giving you the opportunity to see this trait in yourself, a trait that has been unloved or forgotten. The Awakening Crystal holds sacred space for the deep opening of the mind and heart, assisting in dissolving the emotional trigger, allowing us to see the truth of how the emotion was first created. In this process you are able to stop projecting onto others and take back your personal power and responsibility, setting you free from your own emotional chains.

This crystal assists in:
+ deep clearing and healing on an emotional level
+ gaining emotional intelligence
+ releasing and transforming grief, fear and trauma
+ dissolving old wounds of the past
+ understanding the depth of self
+ accepting the dying process
+ understanding your shadow side
+ overcoming addiction
+ healing the nervous system.

Reflection Crystal (Window Crystal)

These pretty crystals are identified by a diamond shape on the face of the crystal. When we connect to the energy of the Reflection Crystal we are given the opportunity to see beyond the illusion, assisting us to see the truth. These crystals are true reflections and windows of our soul and shine back to us our personal divine wisdom from within. Similar to the Awakening Crystal, the Reflection Crystal is a great ally in working with the shadow, allowing us to see into the truth of the situation. The Reflection Crystal supports your journey of following your heart and your divine path here on Earth.

This crystal assists in:

+ truly reflecting your self
+ moving beyond illusion and into your truth
+ deeply reflecting your soul
+ realising and accepting all aspects of yourself.

Ancient Wisdom Crystal (Record Keeper Crystal)

Small triangles on one or more faces of a crystal signify an Ancient Wisdom Crystal. These powerful crystals hold within them the love and wisdom of the universe. Over time they have been programmed with sacred wisdom and knowledge of the future. As this information is ready to be received, these crystals find their way into the hearts and hands of humanity, unlocking the ancient secrets of existence.

Each crystal has a different message to share, as they assist in awakening our planet to a more expanded way of being, living more from a place of love and opening us to a deeper connection to our Divine Mother Earth. To receive this message, simply sit quietly with one of these sacred crystals with the intention of receiving its wisdom. Once you have experienced a connection with an Ancient Wisdom Crystal, you will receive a deep understanding that this knowledge and wisdom already lies within. These crystals are here on Earth to powerfully assist you in reawakening and remembering this ancient wisdom. Ancient Wisdom Crystals activate only when you are ready to awaken. It is possible to have a crystal in your care for years before the small triangles (the distinct markings of the Ancient Wisdom Crystal) show themselves to the receiver.

This crystal assists in:

+ awakening to ancient wisdom
+ finding support and guidance for the future
+ developing a deeper connection to your heart
+ awakening of our divine connection to our planet.

Soul Connection Crystal (Tantric Twin Crystal)

To identify a Soul Connection Crystal look for a crystal that consists of two even and equal points sharing one base. The Soul Connection Crystal holds the energy of pure union and oneness. It consists of two separate Devas living together in harmony within the crystal. This powerful crystal assists in bridging the gap between two people, places, energies or entities, allowing for a deeper and more harmonious relationship and sacred connection between both. It assists us in finding balance within ourselves. When this connection is obtained we can experience a more fulfilling connection with others.

This crystal assists in:

+ realising true union and unity with another
+ creating personal balance
+ realising unity and oneness with self
+ finding inner peace
+ creating peace and harmony
+ enhancing communication
+ bridging the gap
+ connecting to nature and the arts.

Time Travel Crystal
(Time Link Crystal)

Time Travel Crystals are unique to the Crystal Kingdom and are identified by a small or large parallelogram shape along one or more of the faces. This shape can extend up to the left or right of the crystal and sometimes both. Time Travel Crystals create an alignment that connects your soul to aspects of yourself existing in other lifetimes and places within the universe. These crystals assist us in dissolving the illusion of time, allowing us to bring all energy back to the moment for transformation and healing to occur. The parallelograms that extend up to the left of the crystal assist in aligning to the past, allowing for issues of the past to align with the present for healing. The parallelograms that extend to the right assist in aligning with the future, allowing us to master the laws of manifestation and creating a clear path on our journey.

This crystal assists in:

+ breaking through the illusion of time
+ connecting to old wounds of the past for transformation
+ understanding past life therapy
+ projecting into the future
+ manifestation
+ soul retrieval.

Distant Healing Crystal
(Transmitter Crystal)

To identify a Distant Healing Crystal, look for a crystal that has a triangle on the front face, with two seven-edged faces either side. This crystal holds similar properties to the Truth Crystal and also works as a transmitter of energy. Crystals send and receive energy, and the Distant Healing Crystal's geometry amplifies this process. As you connect to this powerful crystal you are assisted in receiving and sending energy from one source to another. It is a great crystal to attune to when sending distance healing and any form of telepathic communication.

This crystal assists in:

✦ prayer
✦ programming
✦ distance healing
✦ telepathic communication
✦ sending and receiving messages
✦ direct connection to the universal love and wisdom
✦ mental clarity.

Balancer Crystal (Tabular Crystal)

These crystals are quite rare and very unique. They are square in shape and quite narrow and their point is flat at the top. The Sacred Geometry of the Balancer Crystal amplifies the properties of the square and resonates the essence of grounding and balance. When attuning to this special crystal, you are connected deeply into our Divine Mother Earth and fully into yourself.

This crystal assists in:

✦ connecting to your higher self
✦ balancing mind, body and spirit
✦ developing overall balance
✦ deeply connecting to the Earth and her healing energy
✦ grounding
✦ creating new beginnings.

Master Deva Crystal (Devic Temple Crystal)

Each crystal has its own soul or Deva that resides within it. The Master Deva Crystal is visible when the spirit or Deva of the crystal has physically manifested itself inside the crystal for the physical eye to see. This is one way for the Deva and consciousness of the crystal to get your attention. Most times the Deva manifests as a form you recognise. For example, if you connect to Angels you will most likely see an Angel in your crystal. These crystals have personal messages for us. When you sit in a sacred space, connecting and tuning in with the crystal, you will receive personal divine guidance and support.

This crystal assists in:

+ gaining support, love and healing from the Crystal Kingdom
+ becoming self-empowered
+ experiencing spiritual awakening
+ gaining insight and wisdom
+ lifting the veils of the world.

Embracing the Shadow Crystal (Phantom Crystal)

This powerful crystal assists you to delve deeply into the shadow self, hence its name. Shadow Crystals have cloudy shapes and sometimes quite solid masses within them that replicate the outer structure or shape of the crystal. This is caused when the crystal stops and starts growing over hundreds of years and the elements in the Earth change, creating a structural image within the crystal. When the elements change quite dramatically the inner image shows as more of a solid mass. They are a powerful and potent crystal to support your journey of looking into the deeper inner aspect of your self. Shadow Crystals assist in bringing light, love and understanding to hidden parts of your being.

This crystal assists in:

+ connecting to your shadow side
+ creating awareness of hidden self
+ peeling back the layers
+ creating balance and harmony
+ letting go of the old and making way for the new.

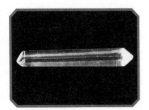

Energiser Crystal (Double Terminator Crystal)

These great crystals consist of terminations or points at both ends of the crystal. This geometry allows for energy to flow freely from one end of the crystal to the other, making them great amplifiers and connectors of energy. You can place these crystals between or around the chakras to assist in creating a powerful energy flow.

This crystal assists in:

+ mental telepathy
+ communication
+ amplifying energy
+ moving stuck energy
+ sending and receiving energy
+ strengthening energy flow.

Ancient Healing Crystal (Laser Wand Crystal)

The Ancient Healing Crystal is a very sacred spiritual tool for many crystal healers. Its points look very similar to those of Quartz crystal but it has many ancient markings on the body and its rough looking surface. It comes to a sharp point at the end where the laser beam of energy exits this powerful crystal. Ancient Healing Crystals hold within them the secrets of crystal healing and have been used by many before us through history. When you are blessed with the opportunity to connect with one of these amazing tools, you will gain much knowledge of the sacred laws of healing. Each crystal has its own unique energy and when aligned to this sacred Deva it will share with you its secrets and how to work with it. For those who know how, these sacred crystals are used as psychic surgery tools where the aura is cut open and energy healing takes place.

This crystal assists in:

+ cutting emotional cords to people
+ creating protective shields
+ performing psychic surgery
+ connecting to ancient wisdom and the laws of healing.

One Love Crystal
(Lemurian Seeded Crystal)

Another one of my favourite crystals from the Crystal Kingdom is the One Love Crystal. These loving beings have three striated sides and three smooth sides, all joining at a point at the top. My personal experience of these amazing crystals is their deep healing energy of unconditional love. Very similar to the Ancient Wisdom Crystal, these crystals also store wisdom and knowledge deep within them. To access this knowledge all you are required to do is connect deeply in sacred space, rubbing your fingers over the striations or lines of the crystal, with the intention of receiving its powerful hidden wisdom and healing.

This crystal assists in:

+ deeply awakening the heart
+ creating deep self-love
+ receiving support and nurturing
+ experiencing all forms of healing
+ opening the third eye
+ accessing ancient wisdom from the past
+ clearing chakras
+ deepening your connection to self and the universe.

One Tribe Crystal
(Barnacle Crystal)

The One Tribe Crystal has other crystals growing off its body. It holds and resonates the energy of tribe, family and community, all living together in harmony. This powerful crystal assists in healing family karma and ancestral patterns, and deepens the bond and connection of all group consciousness.

This crystal assists in:

+ deepening family, tribe or group connections
+ enhancing a sense of community
+ healing family karma and ancestral patterns
+ creating workplace harmony.

Good Fortune Crystal (Grounding Crystal)

This crystal consists of eight edges that make up the main face and is quite a rare specimen in the Crystal Kingdom. Due to its geometry, the energy of this crystal promotes good fortune and abundance in all areas of your life. As the crystal amplifies its structure and geometry, it assists in grounding you to the Earth plane, allowing manifestation to occur with ease and grace.

This crystal assists in:

+ allowing you to receive good fortune
+ creating abundance on all levels
+ initiating new opportunities
+ creating new beginnings
+ finding inspiration
+ grounding.

Chakra Ray Crystal (Rainbow Crystal)

These pretty crystals have the colours of the rainbow manifested within them. They are great to use when doing any type of colour healing. Chakra Ray Crystals also assist in connecting with your inner child aspects, as well as the joy and wonder of life.

This crystal assists in:

+ meditation
+ colour healing
+ chakra balancing
+ dream recall
+ joy, magic and laughter
+ enchantment
+ inner-child healing
+ manifestation.

Golden Door Crystal (Key Crystal)

These crystals are formed when the end of a crystal grows into the outer body of another crystal, leaving an indent the same structure as a termination, most commonly manifesting as a six-sided hole. Golden Door Crystals assist in unlocking hidden knowledge and bringing forth answers to specific questions you may have, opening the golden door of wisdom. To activate this knowledge, sit together in sacred space, creating a deep connection as you ask your desired question. Clear your thoughts and relax as you open your heart and mind to receive the answer.

This crystal assists in:

+ unlocking the doors to healing
+ problem solving
+ accessing hidden information
+ receiving divine wisdom.

Master Healer Crystal (Self-Healed Crystal)

Most crystals grow in clusters within the Earth. Sometimes, due to the Earth's movement, they break off and start their journey on their own.

They then start to heal themselves as many small terminations begin to grow on the broken end of the crystal. In some cases you can see the point where the crystal broke off the cluster as it manifests as a cloudy line.

Master Healer Crystals assist in delving deep within the self, allowing for acceptance and unconditional love as you surrender to the essence of your own soul. Crystals are living beings, forever changing and consistently growing. This must mean that the Master Healer Crystals are always healing themselves, offering and sharing this energy with whoever enters their field.

This crystal assists in:

+ self-healing on all levels — physical, emotional, mental and spiritual
+ connecting to your own healing abilities
+ receiving acceptance and unconditional love
+ overcoming addictions.

Inner Self Crystal (Manifestation Crystal)

Inner Self Crystals have smaller crystals growing within them. These represent your inner aspects and activate the awakening of your inner secrets and gifts, assisting you to look within and honour all of who you are and awaken your true inner wisdom and truth.

This crystal assists in:

+ self-acceptance
+ inner wisdom and truth
+ awakening your gifts.

PART 2

Your personal guide and journey
with the Crystal Kingdom

Creating a sacred union with your crystals

All crystals have their own specific vibration, medicine and energy, and how they relate to us individually can depend on where we are in our life. I am very passionate about encouraging people to have their own experience with the crystals and to bring through their own understanding of how each crystal works. This is why I have created the next section of this workbook — to inspire you and encourage you to have your own healing journey with the Crystal Kingdom.

There are many books on the market that share with us detailed information on each crystal; however, I wanted to inspire you to create your own. I have shared with you my understanding of each crystal, which comes from my own experience and my teachers, as a guide and support for you. As you embark on this journey of getting to know each crystal individually, you will receive deep transformation and healing that will empower you to facilitate your own potent healing with the support of our loving friends from the Earth. This will truly support and awaken you to your own healing experiences, allowing you to accept, love and invoke empowerment in your life, and allowing you to shine in all your totality and divine essence.

What has allowed me to transform and heal so profoundly on my journey is the opportunity to have had my own experiences and awakenings with the Crystal Kingdom and Mother Earth herself.

They are my greatest teachers and such a guidance, love and support in my life. We are all connected deeply to the Earth and to the Crystal Kingdom. There is no separation; we are all one, living and loving here on Earth. The crystals have been put on Earth for many reasons, one being to assist humanity and another being to love us when we have forgotten how to love ourselves. Crystals are truly gifts from Mother Earth and one of her powerful medicines. Some of my teachings have been sparked by my physical teachers here on Earth; however, most of them are from the crystals themselves and my own experiences.

I believe very strongly in having your own experience with the crystals and there is no wrong or right way to do this. It is very much about sitting with a crystal and connecting with the intention of receiving healing or guidance. You will be surprised at what will show up for you. You don't have to do workshops or be on your spiritual path for years to understand and connect to crystals. It is our birthright to share this healing from the Earth and is as simple as sitting in sacred space with your crystals with an open heart and pure intent. I believe we all have the wisdom and knowledge inside us of how to work and connect with the crystals, though it is very unique and special for each individual.

CRYSTAL GUIDE

I encourage you all to sit and share space with your crystals so you too can receive deep healing from these amazing beings of light. I suggest you connect to one crystal at a time. Invite the crystal into your life and start to connect with its energy by sleeping with it under your pillow, meditating with it and carrying it around in your pocket.

You will start to resonate at the same frequency as your crystal and your crystal will activate deep healing within you. The key is to start to become aware of feelings and situations in your life that change, or new awareness that filters in. The healing and transformation that takes place through this time will directly relate to the energy of the crystal. Write your experience in the blank pages below under each crystal as you create your own crystal healing information book just for you. Become aware of how the crystal energy affects you on different levels — emotionally, physically, mentally and spiritually. This awareness will allow you a deeper understanding of your experience with the crystal. As you continue to connect to each crystal you will start to truly embody the crystal light and energy that lies deep within, creating oneness and wholeness in your being. Crystals bring up and amplify our issues, so please remember to be very kind to yourself as you love, nurture, honour and hold yourself through this healing journey gently back to your heart.

Most of the information in the following section has been given to me from the Crystal Kingdom through my own experience. Some of it has been handed down to me from my teachers, as well as from books about crystals. I have only listed the crystals I have personally worked with in my journey.

At times you will notice that crystals have similar properties. Tune into your own intuition as to which crystal best suits you.

Agate

Crystal colour: A range
and variety of earthly
colours consisting of
creams, whites, blacks,
browns, reds and oranges
Related chakras: Base
and sacral

Crystal meaning:
+ Restores, grounds and nurtures the energy field
+ Provides emotional and energetic support
+ Brings in all the divine qualities of Mother Earth
+ Reconnects you to the divine energy flow of the planet
+ Connects you deeply to Mother Earth and opens you to receive
  her powerful healing energy
+ Assists in shamanic journeying to meet the plant and tree Devas
+ Aligns you to their power and spirit animal helpers

Your personal experience with the crystal:

....

....

....

....

....

....

....

Ajoite

Crystal colour: Varieties of blues and greens
Related chakras: Heart and throat

Crystal meaning:

- ✦ Encourages you to connect deeply to your feminine energy
- ✦ Reconnects you to the ancient wisdom of the goddess
- ✦ Reconnects you to your feminine, allowing you to find the strength and wisdom of vulnerability where deep healing occurs

Your personal experience with the crystal:

....

....

....

....

....

....

....

Amazonite

Crystal colour: Bluish green
with white streaks
Related chakras: Solar plexus
and crown

Crystal meaning:
+ Aligns you to your life purpose and encourages you to step
  onto the path with strength and courage
+ Assists you in finding the divine truth in all things
+ Facilitates deep internal reflection
+ Encourages you to come into alignment with your divine will,
  manifesting your heart's desires

Your personal experience with the crystal:

....

....

....

....

....

....

....

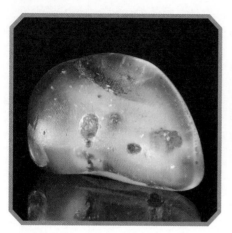

Amber

Crystal colour: Various shades of translucent orange
Related chakras: Base and sacral

Crystal meaning:
+ Allows a deeper connection to the nature and tree spirits
+ Draws disease from the body
+ Assists in dissolving old patterns from the past that are handed down through the DNA and family
+ Assists in creating a deep connection with your ancestors to receive their deep wisdom of life

Your personal experience with the crystal:

....

....

....

....

....

....

....

Amethyst

Crystal colour: Various shades
of translucent purple
Related chakra: Third eye

Crystal meaning:

+ Powerful overall healing crystal, which assists on all levels
+ Balances the left and right hemispheres of the brain, allowing you
  to enter into deep meditation and relaxation
+ Overcomes all types of addiction, bringing awareness and healing
  to the core issue held beneath the addiction and dissolving the
  old patterns
+ Opens you to your psychic abilities
+ Assists wonderfully in dream recall
+ Aids in anxiety and stress relief
+ Soothes energetically and emotionally

Your personal experience with the crystal:

....

....

....

....

....

....

....

Amethyst Awakening (Amethyst Elestial)

Crystal colour: Translucent purpl mixed with smoky quartz
Related chakras: All

Crystal meaning:

+ This beautiful crystal is from the same family as the Awakening Crystal (Elestial); however, is formed with Amethyst
+ One of the most powerful and potent crystals on the planet, here to assist in healing all forms of trauma
+ Helps you to move through lifelong addictions and patterns as you awaken to the core issues that created the need for addiction
+ Assists deep spiritual awakening
+ Supports and enhances emotional intelligence and balances the emotions

Your personal experience with the crystal:

....

....

....

....

....

....

....

Ametrine

Crystal colour: Variety of shades of golds and purples
Related chakras: Solar plexus and third eye

Crystal meaning:

+ Assists in finding a deeper space for meditation and relaxation
+ Opens the third eye and activates your deeper intuition
+ Stimulates and revitalises the brain, enhancing memory
+ Invokes personal power and inner strength

Your personal experience with the crystal:

....

....

....

....

....

....

....

Angelite

Crystal colour: Pale shades of blue and grey
Related chakras: Heart and crown

Crystal meaning:

- ✦ Aligns us to the Angelic Realm, where we receive healing and divine guidance
- ✦ Attracts new people and friendships into your life that align with your higher purpose
- ✦ Connects us to the spirit world and the wisdom it has to offer

Your personal experience with the crystal:

....

....

....

....

....

....

....

Apache Tears

Crystal colour: Black
Related chakras: Base and sacral

Crystal meaning:

+ Assists in dissolving fear of moving forward and of change
+ Allows you to connect to and release any wounds around grief and fear
+ Encourages you to stay centred and grounded and to see the light at the end of the tunnel, bringing hope
+ Assists in overcoming and working through fear of death, accidents and injury

Your personal experience with the crystal:

....

....

....

....

....

....

....

Apatite — Blue

Crystal colour: Blue
Related chakras: Third eye and throat

Crystal meaning:
+ Stimulates and awakens the third eye to receive clearer vision and insight, acting as a powerful visionary stone
+ Aids in positive communication
+ Clears and activates the throat chakra

Your personal experience with the crystal:

....

....

....

....

....

....

....

Apatite — Green

Crystal colour: Green
Related chakra: Heart

Crystal meaning:

+ Overall gentle, supportive healing crystal
+ Awakens the loving essence of the heart
+ Supports in realising and dissolving unhealthy eating patterns
  and addictions

Your personal experience with the crystal:

....

....

....

....

....

....

....

Apophyllite

Crystal colour: Various colours
Related chakras: Sacral, base and crown

Crystal meaning:
+ Assists in healing past life issues, awakening wisdom and understanding of the past
+ Supports in realising and releasing old karmic contracts and connections that no longer serve you
+ Assists in addressing and letting go of karmic issues such as vows of poverty, silence and chastity
+ Deepens your connection to family, promoting healing of family wounds
+ Integrates past life wisdom

Your personal experience with the crystal:

....

....

....

....

....

....

....

Aquamarine

Crystal colour: A range of translucent and opaque blues and aqua
Related chakras: Heart and throat

Crystal meaning:
- ✦ Facilitates clear communication, allowing you to speak truth from the heart, supporting self-expression
- ✦ Assists in connecting to and expressing your own wisdom and knowledge
- ✦ Allows you to find your voice
- ✦ Soothes and calms the emotions
- ✦ Awakens the divine feminine
- ✦ Dissolves the need to feel defensive

Your personal experience with the crystal:

....

....

....

....

....

....

....

Aragonite

Crystal colour: Orange and brown
Related chakras: Base and sacral

Crystal meaning:
+ Brings deep awareness and healing to suppressed emotions
+ Unlocks the hidden aspects of the human psyche
+ Assists in connecting to and understanding the deep wisdom held within the emotional body, bringing about emotional maturity

Your personal experience with the crystal:

....

....

....

....

....

....

....

Aventurine — Green

Crystal colour: Various shades of green
Related chakra: Heart

Crystal meaning:

✦ Assists in connecting to and healing deep wounds and patterns from your childhood
✦ Heals and soothes painful emotions held within the heart
✦ Assists those who are highly sensitive
✦ Nurtures the inner child in times of deep healing
✦ Allows you to acknowledge the loving, joyful child within
✦ Allows you to balance any insensitivity in your life, bringing in a deeper level of compassion
✦ Encourages understanding and insight behind emotional issues

Your personal experience with the crystal:

....

....

....

....

....

....

....

Azurite

Crystal colour: Vibrant ranges of blues
Related chakra: Third eye

Crystal meaning:

+ Connects to and enhances your intuition, creating trust to follow your own guidance
+ Expands your awareness and allows you to see things from a different perspective, allowing for transformation and healing to occur and letting go of old wounds and belief systems
+ Dissolves old belief systems, concepts and misperceptions
+ Opens you to clear vision and insight into your life and others

Your personal experience with the crystal:

....

....

....

....

....

....

....

Bixbite

Crystal colour: Opaque to translucent reds
Related chakra: Sacral

Crystal meaning:

+ Enhances and invokes pleasure and passion within your life, allowing divine union and deep sexual connection to your beloved
+ Invites you to explore the sacredness and power of your sexuality
+ Awakens romantic love and passion
+ Strengthens sexual partnerships and deep connections, creating a sacred space for tantric union
+ Stimulates your sexual energy and invokes healing of any old wounds held from past traumatic experiences around sexual intimacy

Your personal experience with the crystal:

....

....

....

....

....

....

....

Bloodstone

Crystal colour: Dark greens with red and orange spots
Related chakras: Base and sacral

Crystal meaning:
+ Purifies the blood and any blood disorders
+ Restores and nourishes the body
+ Centres, balances and reconnects you to yourself
+ Invites you onto the path of self-love and care
+ Allows you to connect to the innate healing energy of the physical body, supporting it to heal itself

Your personal experience with the crystal:

....

....

....

....

....

....

....

Blue Lace Agate

Crystal colour: Pale blue with white swirls and streaks
Related chakra: Throat

Crystal meaning:

+ Assists in creating clear communication and speaking your divine truth
+ Aids in positive communication
+ Helps you to go with the flow of life
+ Enhances relaxation
+ Opens the throat chakra
+ Enhances self-expression
+ Promotes peaceful flow of expression and calmness

Your personal experience with the crystal:

....

....

....

....

....

....

....

Boji Stones™

Crystal colour: Grey stones. Boji Stones™ always come in pairs. The smooth stone represents the feminine energy and the rough stone represents the masculine energy.
Related chakras: All

Crystal meaning:
+ Creates balance
+ Grounds the spiritual experience into the physical world
+ Supports soul retrieval journey to the inner realms
+ Assists in connecting to your power animal in spirit

Your personal experience with the crystal:

....

....

....

....

....

....

....

Brazilianite

Crystal colour:
A range of translucent
to opaque greens
Related chakras:
Solar plexus and crown

Crystal meaning:
+ Assists in decision making
+ Supports you to become more assertive
+ Enhances intuition
+ Brings inner peace and self-awareness
+ Enhances flexibility in your life
+ Assists in enhancing creative projects
+ Self-empowerment

Your personal experience with the crystal:

....

....

....

....

....

....

....

Brookite

Crystal colour:
Various shades of
browns, golds
and yellows
Related chakras: All

Crystal meaning:

+ Enhances insight into self and others
+ Brings lightness, and uplifts the soul and spirit
+ Assists those who live with fear of the future to live more
  in the present

Your personal experience with the crystal:

....

....

....

....

....

....

....

Bustamite

Crystal colour: Various shades of pink with white
Related chakras: Heart and solar plexus

Crystal meaning:
+ Initiation crystal used in ceremonies and rites of passage.
+ Strengthens belief in self and creates a sense of belonging
+ Heals and transforms issues of the heart (used by shamans in South America for this purpose)

Your personal experience with the crystal:

....

....

....

....

....

....

....

Cacoxenite

Crystal colour: A variety of golds, browns and blacks
Related chakras: Solar plexus and crown

Crystal meaning:
+ Great for enhancing your channelling gifts and abilities
+ Enhances creative ideas and awakens imagination
+ Facilitates high vibrational healing work
+ Journeys with you into the magical realm of spirit
+ Activates new ideas and inspiration in your life

Your personal experience with the crystal:

....

....

....

....

....

....

....

Calcite

Crystal colour: All
Related chakras: All

Crystal meaning:
+ Strengthens the bones and skeletal system
+ Dissolves stress from your life
+ Brings inner peace and tranquillity
+ Calms the mind and balances the heart
+ Facilitates states of deep relaxation and meditation

Your personal experience with the crystal:

....

....

....

....

....

....

....

Calcite — Golden

Crystal colour: Range of opaque yellow to gold
Related chakras: All

Crystal meaning:

+ Opens the crown chakra, and draws in the light and love of the universe
+ Promotes deep relaxation and calms the mind
+ Illuminates the soul
+ Connects you deeply and fully to the wisdom of the cosmos

Your personal experience with the crystal:

....

....

....

....

....

....

....

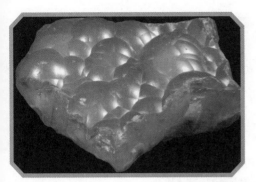

Carnelian

Crystal colour: Various
hues of orange
Related chakra: Sacral

Crystal meaning:
+ Assists in healing and moving through sexual issues, and promotes
  healthy sexual relationships
+ Assists in working through co-dependent issues and letting go
  of negative attachments
+ Assists you to become more independent
+ Transforms anger into motivation and creativity
+ Enhances and awakens creativity within the soul
+ Promotes and assists you to step into courage

Your personal experience with the crystal:

....

....

....

....

....

....

....

Celestite

Crystal colour: Translucent to opaque blue
Related chakras: Throat and crown

Crystal meaning:
+ Facilitates a deep connection to the divine source
+ Encourages acceptance of the flow of life and that all is in divine order
+ Facilitates deep soul healing and transformation
+ Creates a space of peace, calm, tranquillity and deep relaxation
+ Assists connection and communication with the Angelic Realm
+ Soothes the emotions, allowing the heart to open

Your personal experience with the crystal:

....

....

....

....

....

....

....

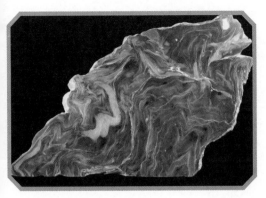

Charoite

Crystal colour:
Various shades of
swirling purples,
whites and black
Related chakras: Third
eye and crown

Crystal meaning:
+ Enhances your psychic abilities and gifts
+ Advances spiritual growth and transformation
+ Allows you to expand through self-denial to see the truth
+ Deepens your journey on the spiritual path
+ Assists in finding the answers that lie within, creating
  self-empowerment

Your personal experience with the crystal:

....

....

....

....

....

....

....

Chiastolite (Andalusite)

Crystal colour: Various hues and shades of golds, browns, oranges, blacks and whites; often seen with a black cross through the crystal
Related chakras: Base and crown

Crystal meaning:

✦ Brings you into alignment with the powerful healing energy and vibration of the Earth
✦ Invokes and anchors the truth of your wisdom to live this in your day-to-day life
✦ Enhances the strength and assurance of your light and wisdom

Your personal experience with the crystal:

....

....

....

....

....

....

....

Chrysanthemum Stone

Crystal colour: Black with white feathers that look like a flower
Related chakra: Solar plexus

Crystal meaning:
+ Bringer and enhancer of abundance
+ Allows you to blossom in your fullness
+ Brings light and understanding to your inner darkness or denial
+ Holds the energy of the ying and yang, facilitating balance and harmony

Your personal experience with the crystal:

....

....

....

....

....

....

....

Chrysoberyl

Crystal colour: Translucent to opaque green
Related chakras: Heart and solar plexus

Crystal meaning:

+ Allows you to attain self-mastery, letting your true essence shine through
+ Creates truth, confidence and freedom in your life
+ Aligns the divine heart and mind to a higher purpose
+ Assists you to find the inner strength and determination to follow your passion, moving out of the old, comfortable place and to bathing and shining in the new of your totality
+ Encourages you to listen to your inner voice
+ Encourages you to embrace personal wisdom and enhances personal growth

Your personal experience with the crystal:

....

....

....

....

....

....

....

Chrysocolla

Crystal colour: Various shades of greens and blues
Related chakras: Solar plexus and heart

Crystal meaning:

+ Assists in bringing eternal love and connection to the divine feminine
+ Assists in connecting to the sacred goddess within
+ Brings old emotion to the surface for transmutation in a gentle, supporting way, letting go of old trauma
+ Encourages honouring of self and others' choices and decisions
+ Assists in powerful, clear communication of our feelings, creating unconditional love and understanding of situations

Your personal experience with the crystal:

....

....

....

....

....

....

....

Chrysoprase

Crystal colour: Green
Related chakra: Heart

Crystal meaning:
+ Encourages appropriate self-discipline in your life
+ Addresses and assists in bringing awareness and healing to self-sacrificing behaviours
+ Assists in resolving inner conflict and turmoil
+ Assists in nurturing, love and support of self
+ Helps in healing old pain residue from abusive and toxic situations

Your personal experience with the crystal:

....

....

....

....

....

....

....

Cinnabar

Crystal colour: Various shades of red and browns with white
Related chakra: Crown

Crystal meaning:
+ Allows you to get out of your own way
+ Allows you to trust in the flow of life and what it has to offer
+ Invites the energy of joy and magic into your life on all levels
+ Encourages you to lighten up and remember to play and have fun in life
+ Invites you to choose a positive outlook on life

Your personal experience with the crystal:

....

....

....

....

....

....

....

Citrine

Crystal colour: Yellows and golds
Related chakra: Solar plexus

Crystal meaning:
+ Purification crystal on all levels
+ Assists in manifesting wealth and abundance
+ Brings healthy positive energy into your life
+ Shifts old patterns of lack and negativity
+ Brings in the joy and magic of life

Your personal experience with the crystal:

....

....

....

....

....

....

....

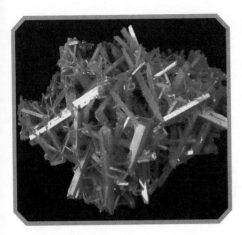

Crocoite

Crystal colour: Vibrant orange
Related chakra: Sacral

Crystal meaning:

+ Has aphrodisiac qualities
+ Activates the Kundalini energy
+ Invokes your deep sexual and life force energy
+ Deepens our connection to our sensuality
+ Assists in sexual healing
+ Enhances Tantric union
+ Enhances sexual confidence
+ Assists you in expressing your creativity

Your personal experience with the crystal:

....

....

....

....

....

....

....

Chrysotile

Crystal colour: Green with white shimmery lines
Related chakras: Base and crown

Crystal meaning:

+ Allows you to connect deeply with your power animal in spirit
+ Allows deep connection to the inner worlds
+ Assists in awakening the wisdom of the animal kingdom and the deep healing it has to share

Your personal experience with the crystal:

....

....

....

....

....

....

....

Cuprite

Crystal colour: Deep red
Related chakras: Base and sacral

Crystal meaning:

✦ Supports exploring the shadow self; also healing deep issues related to the sacred feminine as you are supported to enter into your own personal healing cave for self-reflection
✦ Provides access to sacred ancient knowledge of the feminine; used also for rites of passage
✦ Supports and holds you as you enter into the void, a journey that needs to be taken for deep transformational healing
✦ Supports you to feel like you belong here on Earth

Your personal experience with the crystal:

....

....

....

....

....

....

....

Danburite

Crystal colour: Translucent to opaque
Related chakra: Crown

Crystal meaning:
+ Deepens connection to your higher self
+ Deepens connection to your soul purpose and potential
+ Creates a deep sense of stillness and inner peace
+ Connects you with your limitless potential to create your
  deepest desires
+ Enhances your spirituality, psychic development and
  channelling abilities
+ Facilitates access to the higher realms and connection to
  the Angels and ascended masters

Your personal experience with the crystal:

....

....

....

....

....

....

....

Diamond

Crystal colour: Translucent to opaque yellows and golds
Related chakra: Heart

Crystal meaning:
- Brings light to any situation
- Dispels anger and promotes love and peace
- Promotes deep connection and intimacy with your partner, creating a loving, divine union
- Deepens intimate relationships
- Encourages you to connect deeply to your sensuality
- Promotes unconditional love and deep commitment
- Brings the awareness that we are all one and all love
- Allows you to feel safe in your vulnerability

Your personal experience with the crystal:

....

....

....

....

....

....

....

Diopside

Crystal colour: Various hues of green
Related chakra: Heart

Crystal meaning:

+ Assists in connecting to the heart of Mother Earth, realising she is our true divine mother, receiving healing energy around our mother issues
+ Allows an opening to receive and nurture yourself
+ Brings awareness to deep-seated rejection issues that stem from birth or early childhood
+ Assists in releasing fear and abandonment
+ Assists you in identifying trauma carried from the womb
+ Assists in healing issues in connecting and bonding with your inner child or your own children

Your personal experience with the crystal:

....

....

....

....

....

....

....

Dioptase

Crystal colour: Emerald green
Related chakra: Heart

Crystal meaning:

+ Heals the inner realms of the wounded heart and enhances openness in your life
+ Transmutes and heals emotional pain and old wounds of the past, as the green healing ray penetrates deep into the heart chakra
+ Allows you to release and dissolve sadness in your life
+ Encourages you to let down the walls of anger, bitterness and resistance, and embrace love and connection with others
+ Helps release emotionally defensive behaviours and opens the heart for healing

Your personal experience with the crystal:

....

....

....

....

....

....

....

Dumortierite

Crystal colour: Variety of blues, white and black
Related chakras: Throat and crown

Crystal meaning:

+ Allows you to communicate divine spiritual teachings in a practical and grounded way so that others will understand clearly
+ Supports you to integrate and believe in the wisdom and knowledge received from your higher self
+ Assists you in addressing and releasing any old blockages around expressing your spiritual truths and wisdom

Your personal experience with the crystal:

....

....

....

....

....

....

....

Emerald

Crystal colour: Opaque to translucent greens
Related chakra: Heart

Crystal meaning:
+ Promotes Divine Love and compassion
+ Assists in staying connected to the wisdom of the heart
+ Deeply activates the heart chakra and assists in creating intimacy with self, others and the divine
+ Assists in letting go of old connections and superficial relationships that no longer serve you
+ Invokes the magical healing energy of the dragon
+ Releases the need to please others
+ Brings in positive self-image and supports you to feel good about yourself

Your personal experience with the crystal:

....

....

....

....

....

....

....

Eudialyte

Crystal colour: Ruby red mixed with grey and black
Related chakras: Solar plexus and sacral

Crystal meaning:
+ Restores your self-respect
+ Assists in finding a deep respect and honour for yourself
+ Enhances self-acceptance
+ Teaches you to put yourself first in a healthy way
+ Awakens your deep passion and spark for life

Your personal experience with the crystal:

....

....

....

....

....

....

....

Fairy Stone

Crystal colour: Light grey
to dark grey stone
Related chakras: All

Crystal meaning:

+ Sacred stone to the Native American tribes found in Northern Quebec, Canada; also a stone of magic and good luck
+ Enhances fertility
+ Assists in healing trauma created in the womb
+ Offers protection
+ Brings good health and prosperity

Your personal experience with the crystal:

....

....

....

....

....

....

....

Fire Agate

Crystal colour: Variety of vibrant rich colours of red, orange, blacks, creams, browns, greens, blues, golds and yellows
Related chakra: Sacral

Crystal meaning:
+ Assists in dissolving blocks around your artistic gifts and talents, allowing you to open and shine in deep passion and creativity
+ Enhances self-confidence
+ Encourages you to get in touch with your dynamic nature
+ Assists you to move forward with passion and positivity
+ Deepens your passion and spark for life, fuelling your internal flame and invoking inspiration
+ Stimulates and balances sexual energy

Your personal experience with the crystal:

....

....

....

....

....

....

....

Fluorite

Crystal colour: Range of purple, green and yellow
Related chakras: All

Crystal meaning:
+ Allows you to open to new knowledge and stimulates learning
+ Stimulates the mental body and enhances memory and decision making
+ Assists in releasing unwanted thought patterns and distractions
+ Supports you when you are experiencing emotional confusion to gain a clear perspective
+ Releases constant worry and invites you into the present moment
+ Aids in vision and deep insight
+ Balances the mind and mental body

Your personal experience with the crystal:

....

....

....

....

....

....

....

Fulgurite

Crystal colour: Whites, browns and creams
Related chakras: All

Crystal meaning:

+ Activates and facilitates the Kundalini activation within the physical body
+ Powerfully and quickly clears old emotional patterns
+ Promotes deep transformation

Your personal experience with the crystal:

....

....

....

....

....

....

....

Galena

Crystal colour: Grey to silver
Related chakras: All

Crystal meaning:
+ Very strong grounding stone, creating courage and strength
+ Promotes and supports soul retrieval journeys
+ Balances and heals the nervous system and balances blood pressure

Your personal experience with the crystal:

....

....

....

....

....

....

....

Garnet

Crystal colour: Deep red, black, brown, yellow and green
Related chakras: All

Crystal meaning:
+ Promotes balance and stability in your life
+ Enhances personal power
+ Creates overall health and wellbeing
+ Allows you to dissolve commitment issues and create deeper, fulfilling relationships
+ Encourages you to connect deeply to your sensuality
+ Helps you address issues of self-doubt
+ Teaches you to trust and believe in yourself
+ Connects to and draws up the healing energy of the Earth

Your personal experience with the crystal:

....

....

....

....

....

....

....

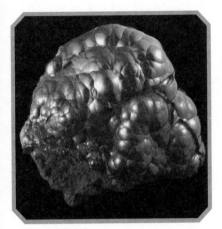

Goethite

Crystal colour: Various hues of brownish black, yellows and reds
Related chakra: Base

Crystal meaning:
+ Accesses the sacred wisdom that lies within the Earth
+ Balances, stimulates and heals the emotional body
+ Allows you to feel and deal with your grief
+ Overcomes lack of faith in self and humanity
+ Supports you to overcome helplessness

Your personal experience with the crystal:

....

....

....

....

....

....

....

Heliodor

Crystal colour: Translucent to opaque gold and yellow
Related chakra: Solar plexus

Crystal meaning:
+ Allows you to take more responsibility in your life
+ Flexibility and spontaneity, and trust in the universal order and divine plan
+ Allows you to let go of control created by ego and allows more flexibility and motivation in your life
+ Encourages self-empowerment and strength

Your personal experience with the crystal:

....

....

....

....

....

....

....

Hematite

Crystal colour: Various shades of
black to grey
Related chakra: Base

Crystal meaning:
+ Purifies and cleanses
+ Cleanses the blood and assists in healing blood disorders
+ Grounds and connects to the centre of the Earth, enhancing
  manifestation skills
+ Promotes balance
+ Encourages gentle healing after shock or trauma
+ Assists in integration of sudden and unexpected change

Your personal experience with the crystal:

....

....

....

....

....

....

....

Herkimer Diamond

Crystal colour:
Translucent to opaque
Related chakras: Heart
and crown

Crystal meaning:
+ Invokes your dynamic personality and vibrancy
+ Allows you to shine in your totality and magnificence
+ Draws in vibrant energy
+ Energetically detoxifies
+ Activates inspiration and new ideas, and clears creative blocks
+ Sweeps the mind clear of clutter
+ Revitalises the spirit

Your personal experience with the crystal:

....

....

....

....

....

....

....

Hiddenite

Crystal colour:
Translucent to
opaque green
Related chakra: Heart

Crystal meaning:
+ Crystal of deep gratitude
+ Allows you to realise that gratitude is the key to receiving
+ Opens the heart and assists in dissolving any judgments in your life
+ Allows you to create a sense of satisfaction and fulfilment in your life
+ Helps shift unhealthy patterns such as comfort eating and other
  addictive behaviours
+ Encourages appreciation for life and yourself

Your personal experience with the crystal:

....

....

....

....

....

....

....

Jade

Crystal colour: Various shades of green
Related chakra: Heart

Crystal meaning:
+ Creates abundance and good fortune
+ Promotes positive thinking and self-expression
+ Creates inner harmony
+ Promotes trust in the creative power of the universe
+ Encourages faith in the ebb and flow of life
+ Enhances devotion to yourself and your life

Your personal experience with the crystal:

....

....

....

....

....

....

....

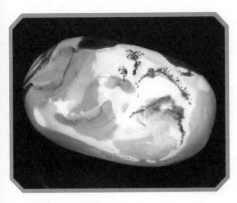

Jasper — Mookite

Crystal colour: Various earthly colours such as oranges, reds, purples, browns, yellows and creams
Related chakras: Base and sacral

Crystal meaning:
+ Used in ceremonies and rituals
+ Encourages deep connection to the wisdom and ancestors of Australia
+ Helps release deep emotions such as fear and anger
+ Assists in your journey into the spirit world and Dreamtime
+ Helps us receive deep healing from the Earth
+ Reconnects us to the heart of the Earth
+ Grounds and protects us
+ Assists in healing issues related to the liver

Your personal experience with the crystal:

....

....

....

....

....

....

....

Jasper — Ocean

Crystal colour: Various colours of green, red, orange, yellow, cream, white and brown
Related chakras: Base, sacral and heart

Crystal meaning:

+ Assists in healing any suppressed emotions, bringing them to the surface for transformation
+ Allows you to open and receive
+ Connects us to the healing energy of the ocean
+ Assists in the release of deeply held, long-term anger, rage, resentment and grief
+ Heals current emotional trauma
+ Helps to dissolve the emotional walls of protection that prevent true healing

Your personal experience with the crystal:

....

....

....

....

....

....

....

Jasper — Red

Crystal colour: Red
Related chakra: Base

Crystal meaning:

+ Sacred stone used in ceremonies and rituals for protection
+ Connects us to Mother Earth and draws her healing energy up into the body, creating strength and balance
+ Connects us with our ancestors
+ Assists us to set healthy boundaries
+ Awakens ancient memories
+ Assists in overcoming deep-seated fear of abandonment
+ Assists in letting go of controlling behaviours

Your personal experience with the crystal:

....

....

....

....

....

....

....

Jet

Crystal colour: Black
Related chakras: Base and sacral

Crystal meaning:

+ Assists in entering the void where we obtain our true depth of self, gaining understanding and power
+ Assists in embracing disowned aspects of self
+ Stimulates and awakens the Kundalini
+ Helps to clear and dissolve energetic residue within the head, clearing headaches

Your personal experience with the crystal:

....

....

....

....

....

....

....

Kunzite

Crystal colour: Various hues of pink, purple, cream and white
Related chakra: Heart

Crystal meaning:
+ Connects you to your own infinite source of love
+ Allows the heart to expand as you enter into the flow of giving and receiving
+ Activates the wisdom of love in the deeper chambers of the heart
+ Allows you to heal from abandonment and rejection as you find your own source of deep love from within
+ Opens and aligns the heart chakra to Divine Love
+ Assists in dissolving deeply held pain and resentment
+ Brings awareness to behaviours and patterns of self-betrayal

Your personal experience with the crystal:

....

....

....

....

....

....

....

Kyanite — Blue

Crystal colour: Blue with strips of silver mica
Related chakra: Throat

Crystal meaning:
+ Deepens self-awareness
+ Expands your consciousness, creating new opportunities in life
+ Allows you to let go of old emotions, allowing you to express the old and make way for the new
+ Helps you in letting go and moving with the ebb and flow of life
+ Assists in connecting to your voice with free-flowing expression

Your personal experience with the crystal:

....

....

....

....

....

....

....

Labradorite

Crystal colour: Greys and silver with vibrant blues and greens
Related chakras: Third eye and crown

Crystal meaning:

+ Allows you to connect to the mystery and magic of life
+ Assists in awakening the magic of your soul
+ Brings deep awareness of our spiritual knowledge, allowing it to manifest in your day-to-day life
+ Brings spiritual insight
+ Supports you to integrate spiritual experiences into the physical world
+ Opens and activates the third eye

Your personal experience with the crystal:

....

....

....

....

....

....

....

Lapis Lazuli

Crystal colour: Various shades
of blue with gold streaks
and speckles
Related chakras: Third eye
and crown

Crystal meaning:

+ Powerful spiritual initiation stone, awakening spiritual wisdom
  and knowledge from within
+ Opens you to clairvoyance
+ Supports past life awareness and healing of any karmic patterns
+ Attunes you to your ancient wisdom
+ Enhances psychic gifts and awareness
+ Supports you in connecting to your deep spiritual truths
+ Severs karmic ties

Your personal experience with the crystal:

....

....

....

....

....

....

....

Larimar

Crystal colour: Various shades of bluish greens and white
Related chakras: Throat and heart

Crystal meaning:
+ Empowers the goddess within all of us, allowing for deep healing of our feminine
+ Balances the fire and water element, soothing the emotions and setting us free from anger and frustration
+ Calms and stabilises erratic emotional states
+ Brings comfort and support in cases of heightened sensitivity
+ Assists reactive individuals to express from a place of self-empowerment
+ Relaxes the nerves

Your personal experience with the crystal:

....

....

....

....

....

....

....

Lepidolite

Crystal colour: Pinks and
light purples
Related chakras: Third eye
and sacral

Crystal meaning:

- ✦ Assists in letting go of old critical judgments of self
- ✦ Assists in transitioning from the old way of being to creating
  a new path of self-empowerment
- ✦ Allows us to see the truth and live in the moment
- ✦ Assists us in surrendering and creating more peace and serenity
  in our life
- ✦ Supports perfectionists in letting go
- ✦ Soothes the inner critic
- ✦ Releases unrealistic expectations of self and others

Your personal experience with the crystal:

....

....

....

....

....

....

....

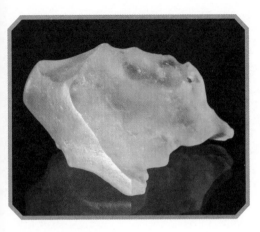

Libyan Gold Tektite

Crystal colour: Opaque yellow and gold
Related chakra: Crown

Crystal meaning:

+ Powerful manifestation crystal
+ Assists in connecting to light beings from other galaxies and dimensions
+ Releases fear of the unknown, allowing more trust in your life
+ Dissolves fear around extraterrestrial beings

Your personal experience with the crystal:

....

....

....

....

....

....

....

Malachite

Crystal colour: Green with black swirls
Related chakras: All

Crystal meaning:

✦ Deep physical healing crystal that penetrates into all levels of your being and promotes overall healing
✦ Powerful crystal that assists in healing broken bones, bruises and all physical disease
✦ Opens and expands the heart chakra, allowing the power of love to dissolve deeply held resentment and sadness stored within the body
✦ Excellent to work with after meditation or healing to integrate the experience
✦ Eases deep heartache

Your personal experience with the crystal:

....

....

....

....

....

....

....

Malachite and Azurite

Crystal colour: Green with black swirls mixed with vibrant blue
Related chakras: All

Crystal meaning:
+ This crystal is Malachite and Azurite growing together to create a powerful synergy
+ Holds the energetic properties of both Malachite and Azurite, with both crystals amplifying the other to create a powerful overall healing crystal on all levels.
+ Activates the blue and green rays of peace and healing
+ Refer to Malachite and Azurite for properties

Your personal experience with the crystal:

....

....

....

....

....

....

....

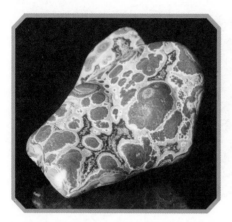

Malachite and Chrysocolla

Crystal colour: Green with black swirls and various shades of greens and blues
Related chakras: All

Crystal meaning:

+ This crystal is Malachite and Chrysocolla growing together to create powerful synergy
+ Holds the energetic properties of both Malachite and Chrysocolla, with both crystals amplifying each other to create a powerful overall healing crystal on all levels
+ Refer to Malachite and Chrysocolla for properties

Your personal experience with the crystal:

....

....

....

....

....

....

....

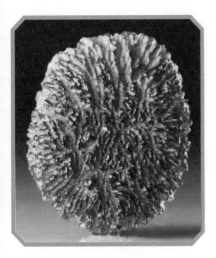

Moldavite

Crystal colour: Opaque
bottle green
Related chakras: Crown

Crystal meaning:
+ Powerful crystal which assists in connecting and communicating
  with dimensional light beings from other universes and planes
  of existence
+ Brings deep spiritual connection to awakening and healing
+ Supports astral travelling into different time, places and dimensions

Your personal experience with the crystal:

....

....

....

....

....

....

....

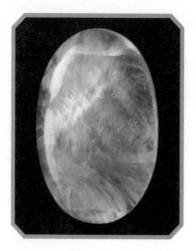

Moonstone

Crystal colour: Varieties of white, pearly and cream hues
Related chakras: Sacral and heart

Crystal meaning:

+ Connects us deeply to our feminine and heals any imbalances in this area
+ Enhances fertility, planting new seeds, ideas and inspirations
+ Creates new beginnings, new directions and creativity
+ Connects us to the energy of the moon and her cycles, bringing us into balance and the ebb and flow of life
+ Encourages us to open to intimacy
+ Assists in birthing new projects and creations

Your personal experience with the crystal:

....

....

....

....

....

....

....

Morganite

Crystal colour: Opaque to translucent pink
Related chakra: Heart

Crystal meaning:
+ Creates a sacred space to assist moving deeply into the inner chambers of the heart, connecting to the love of the divine
+ Enhances love of all aspects of self
+ Allows you to heal old relationship wounds as the heart opens and healing occurs
+ Creates a sacred space to heal any wounds or disconnection between two souls in divine relationship
+ Assists in rapid heart healing

Your personal experience with the crystal:

....

....

....

....

....

....

....

Natrolite

Crystal colour: Translucent to opaque
yellow, brown and cream
Related chakras: Third eye and crown

Crystal meaning:
+ Assists spiritual awakening
+ Deepens spiritual connection
+ Supports and integrates energetic and vibrational shifts
+ Brings stability and energetic balance

Your personal experience with the crystal:

....

....

....

....

....

....

....

Nirvana Quartz

Crystal colour: Opaque pink
Related chakras: Heart and crown

Crystal meaning:

+ Connects deeply to the heart chakra and allows for any old wounds to be released softly and gently as you love and nurture yourself through the process
+ Assists in deepening feelings of self-worth and acceptance
+ Connects into the wisdom and sacred energy of the Himalayas where this beautiful crystal is birthed, connecting into the energy of oneness
+ Assists deep meditation and stillness
+ Allows you to open and blossom like a lotus flower, embodying peace and tranquillity

Your personal experience with the crystal:

....

....

....

....

....

....

....

Nuummite

Crystal colour: Black with gold and brown streaks
Related chakras: All

Crystal meaning:
+ Stone of the warrior and shaman
+ Supports us on the journey into our shadow self, creating a sacred space to obtain deep wisdom, strength and courage
+ Increases strength and endurance during difficult times
+ Assists us on the journey to self-mastery
+ Assists the journey to self-mastery

Your personal experience with the crystal:

....

....

....

....

....

....

....

Obsidian — Black

Crystal colour: Black
Related chakras: Base

Crystal meaning:

+ Powerful cleanser of negative energy in the body and energy field
+ Draws to the surface any unresolved issues for release and healing
+ Dissolves destructive patterns
+ Allows old habits and traits to surface so you can love and accept the self in its totality
+ Allows you to enter into the void to receive wisdom and knowledge from your shadow side
+ Supports you through the dark night of the soul
+ Brings deep life revelations and realisations
+ Brings rapid positive change

Your personal experience with the crystal:

....

....

....

....

....

....

....

Opal

Crystal colour: Range of opaque colours
Related chakras: All

Crystal meaning:

+ Allows you to experience the love, joy and pure essence of your soul
+ Used in Aboriginal Dreamtime ceremonies to support and strengthen vision quests
+ Activates the thymus and allows you to enter into a sacred space of love and joy
+ Enhances joy, spontaneity and flow
+ Encourages you to engage in the vibrant energy of life

Your personal experience with the crystal:

....

....

....

....

....

....

....

Orpiment

Crystal colour: Deep orange surrounded by gold and yellow shards
Related chakra: Sacral

Crystal meaning:
+ Manifestation crystal
+ Allows you to connect to new projects and ideas
+ Awakens new projects and ideas
+ Aligns to success in your life
+ Assists in holding and staying focused on clear positive intentions
+ Supports strength and commitment to self

Your personal experience with the crystal:

....

....

....

....

....

....

....

Peridot

Crystal colour: Opaque green
Related chakra: Heart

Crystal meaning:

+ A great crystal to assist us in connecting to the nature spirits
  and fairy realm
+ A powerful crystal for attracting abundance
+ Allows us to feel deep gratitude in our life
+ Enhances love, marriage and romantic ceremonies
+ Deepens love, loyalty and commitment
+ Enhances our ability to experience both inner and outer beauty
+ Activates the higher heart chakra, allowing us to live in a constant
  state of love

Your personal experience with the crystal:

....

....

....

....

....

....

....

Petrified Wood

Crystal colour:
Crystallised wood
Related chakra: Base

Crystal meaning:
+ Strong grounding stone and centring crystal
+ Assists in connecting you with the tree spirits to receive deep wisdom and healing from our ancestors
+ Awakens the deep knowledge that lies within the blood and bones of our ancestry
+ Assists in realising any old ancestral karma brought down through the bloodline

Your personal experience with the crystal:

....

....

....

....

....

....

....

Phenacite

Crystal colour: Opaque to translucent
Related chakras: Third eye and crown

Crystal meaning:
+ Used in spiritual awakening, initiation and ceremony
+ Opens and activates the crown chakra, allowing you to access and align to universal love and wisdom
+ Helps you receive divine guidance and direction from your higher self
+ Enhances your spiritual journey
+ Connects you to the higher realms of consciousness
+ Assists in healing spiritual traumas

Your personal experience with the crystal:

....

....

....

....

....

....

....

Pietersite

Crystal colour: Range of many earthly colours like browns, golds, reds, purples and yellows
Related chakra: Crown

Crystal meaning:
+ Is the key to Heaven, enhancing your connection to higher spiritual wisdom and knowledge
+ Frees you from the entrapments of the mind
+ Assists in accessing the Akashic Records
+ Creates clarity and inner strength
+ Supports your spiritual awakening

Your personal experience with the crystal:

....

....

....

....

....

....

....

Prehnite

Crystal colour: Opaque green
with white
Related chakras: Heart

Crystal meaning:

+ Connects us deeply into the heart of Mother Earth where we
  receive deep healing and nurturing
+ Heals the deep inner realms of the heart, allowing you to feel
  safe to love again
+ Supports in the rebuilding of trust in a relationship
+ Encourages you to believe in yourself and your dreams
+ Activates the wisdom of the heart and mind

Your personal experience with the crystal:

....

....

....

....

....

....

....

Purpurite

Crystal colour: Purplish silver
Related chakras: Third eye
and crown

Crystal meaning:

+ Visionary stone
+ Awakens awareness of spiritual truths
+ Activates deep personal insights
+ Opens you to your destiny
+ Builds trust in self and intuition

Your personal experience with the crystal:

....

....

....

....

....

....

....

Pyrite

Crystal colour: Silver, gold and grey
Related chakras: Third eye and base

Crystal meaning:

+ Anchors the mental body into the physical plane and assists in calming the mind, dissolving mind chatter
+ Enhances brain function and memory
+ Helps calm excessive thinking and irrational fears
+ Allows you to create action and manifestation in your life

Your personal experience with the crystal:

....

....

....

....

....

....

Pyromorphite

Crystal colour: Lime green
Related chakras: Solar plexus and heart

Crystal meaning:

+ Assists in creating more patience, allowing for a deeper level of tolerance and understanding
+ Deepens your intuition and gut feelings
+ Encourages assertiveness and courage
+ Supports you to stand up for yourself
+ Addresses issues of low self-esteem
+ Promotes a deeper belief in and respect for your self

Your personal experience with the crystal:

....

....

....

....

....

....

....

Quartz — Clear

Crystal colour: Opaque to translucent
Related chakras: All

Crystal meaning:
+ Amplifies, stores, transmutes, transcends and retains energy
+ Moves light and energy into and out of the body as it clears and cleanses the energy field
+ Motivates
+ Enhances and amplifies intentions
+ Amplifies and deepens the love and wisdom from the universe
+ Allows a deep sense of clarity in your life

Your personal experience with the crystal:

....

....

....

....

....

....

Rhodochrosite

Crystal colour: Pink
with white swirls
Related chakras: Heart

Crystal meaning:

+ Powerful crystal for self-healing and acceptance
+ Brings in the energy of unconditional love to assist in balancing,
  soothing and healing the emotions
+ Creates a deeper belief in your life, enhancing self-love
  and compassion
+ Supports those who are emotionally overwhelmed
+ Assists you to surrender and let go
+ Assists you to become more self-aware
+ Supports you to make balanced, rational decisions

Your personal experience with the crystal:

....

....

....

....

....

....

....

Rhodonite

Crystal colour: Various pinks, reds and greys
Related chakras: Solar plexus and heart

Crystal meaning:

+ Crystal for self-reflection
+ Connects to and follows your inner voice
+ Connect to your inner voice
+ Powerful meditation crystal, allowing you to go within, creating a deeper awareness of self and allowing you to access personal power
+ Helps to calm jealous and possessive feelings in relationships

Your personal experience with the crystal:

....

....

....

....

....

....

....

Rose Quartz

Crystal colour: Various shades of pink
Related chakra: Heart

Crystal meaning:

+ Crystal for deepening self-love and acceptance
+ Activates deep love and peace within the heart
+ Bringing conditional love to the emotions, activating the wisdom of the heart
+ Enhances compassion, gentleness and nurturing of your soul
+ Brings self-fulfilment and inner peace
+ Assists in creating more patience and understanding in your life
+ Gently assists you to feel your inner emotions
+ Supports and nurtures those going through divorce and separation

Your personal experience with the crystal:

....

....

....

....

....

....

....

Ruby

Crystal colour: Deep shades of red
Related chakra: Sacral

Crystal meaning:
+ Dissolves deep trauma and grief within the body and allows for you to love yourself through the challenges of life
+ Enhances passion in all areas of life
+ Deepens your sensual aspects of self, allowing you to receive a flow of life-force energy and creativity
+ Helps to recognise the source of fear and anxiety

Your personal experience with the crystal:

....

....

....

....

....

....

....

Rutilated Quartz

Crystal colour: Quartz with fine hairs inside the crystal
Related chakras: Sacral and crown

Crystal meaning:

+ Assists in healing issues related to family, handed down through the DNA
+ Assists in the release of fear and anxiety stemming from childhood memories
+ Transforms and shifts conflicts within the family unit

Your personal experience with the crystal:

....

....

....

....

....

....

....

Scolecite

Crystal colour: White
Related chakra: Crown

Crystal meaning:
+ Enhances a deep sacred space of meditation and relaxation
+ Promotes inner peace and tranquillity
+ Supports us in the awakening of our inner wisdom
+ Allows us to access deeply held subconscious memories
  for transformation
+ Assists in purification and illumination of the soul

Your personal experience with the crystal:

....

....

....

....

....

....

....

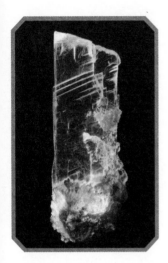

Selenite

Crystal colour: White to translucent with striations
Related chakra: Crown

Crystal meaning:
+ Powerful crystal working as a vacuum cleaner to purify and cleanse the aura
+ Opens and stimulates the crown chakra and brings in the divine light of the cosmos, balancing the chakras
+ Encourages you to take powerful action in your life
+ Allows you to move forward in strength
+ Connects to your higher self and 'I am' presence
+ Shields the aura from any unwanted influences
+ Detoxifies the energy field

Your personal experience with the crystal:

....

....

....

....

....

....

....

Seraphinite

Crystal colour: Green, black and white swirls
Related chakras: All

Crystal meaning:

+ Quickens your spiritual learning
+ Assists in connecting to the Angels and guides
+ Assists in understanding and release of old emotional patterns, allowing transformation in your life
+ Enhances clarity and purification
+ Brings new vision and direction
+ Renews your sense of purpose and life mission

Your personal experience with the crystal:

....

....

....

....

....

....

....

Serpentine

Crystal colour: Green and black
Related chakras: Base, sacral and heart

Crystal meaning:

+ Has deep connection to Peru and the ancient wisdom of its tribes and their healing ways
+ Powerful healing energy that penetrates on all levels
+ Stimulates the Kundalini energy to be released within the body
+ Invokes deep transformation, and brings in the medicine of the snake and life-force energy

Your personal experience with the crystal:

....

....

....

....

....

....

....

Shaman Stone

Crystal colour:
Roundish, grey,
iron-coated sandstone
Related chakras: All

Crystal meaning:

+ A powerful ally for shamans
+ Assists and facilitates shamanic and soul retrieval journeys into the three worlds
+ Has deep connection to the medicine and wisdom of the Earth
+ Awakens your inner shamanic power and wisdom
+ Connects to your ancestors and their wisdom
+ Assists in realising unwanted spirits and energetic attachments

Your personal experience with the crystal:

....

....

....

....

....

....

....

Shattuckite

Crystal colour: Various
shades of blues and greens
Related chakras: Heart,
throat and crown

Crystal meaning:

+ Invokes the wisdom of the inner teacher
+ Opens the heart to allow you to share wisdom from a place of love
+ Supports you to share the divine wisdom of the universe
+ Connects and encourages you to your teacher guides in the
  higher realms

Your personal experience with the crystal:

....

....

....

....

....

....

....

Shiva Lingam

Crystal colour: Brown, red, grey egg-shaped stone
Related chakra: Sacral

Crystal meaning:
+ Assists in severing old energy cords and attachments to previous sexual partners and experiences
+ Activates fertility, new beginnings and rebirth
+ Connects you to the energy of the divine masculine, invoking the energy of Shiva

Your personal experience with the crystal:

....

....

....

....

....

....

....

Smoky Quartz

Crystal colour: Smoky coloured quartz
Related chakras: Base and sacral

Crystal meaning:
+ Powerful grounding crystal
+ Enhances a deep connection to Mother Earth and her healing vibration
+ Facilitates your connection back to nature and allows you to receive the deep peace and tranquillity that comes with such an experience
+ Transforms negative energy and thought forms, allowing you to feel rejuvenated
+ Supports you in dissolving fears and limitations
+ Assists you in moving through panic attacks and anxiety
+ Reminds you to breathe deeply and embrace life

Your personal experience with the crystal:

....

....

....

....

....

....

....

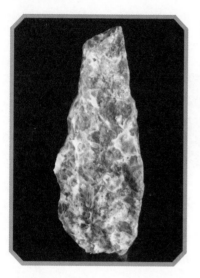

Sodalite

Crystal colour: Various shades of blue, white and black
Related chakras: Solar plexus and throat

Crystal meaning:
+ Creates self-acceptance and enhances self-worth
+ Deepens intuition
+ Encourages you to believe in the divine essence of your soul
+ Assists in healing your self-esteem and self-worth issues
+ Enhances self-confidence
+ Soothes, calms and heals the soul from any trauma

Your personal experience with the crystal:

....

....

....

....

....

....

....

Spirit Quartz

Crystal colour: Range of lavender, pink and white
Related chakras: All

Crystal meaning:

+ Opens you to your natural gifts and talents related to music and sound
+ Enhances your creative musical passions and pursuits
+ Opens you to the music of the cosmos
+ Connects you to the fairy realm and nature spirits, creating a sense of magic in your life
+ Balances the chakras and energy field, creating wellbeing
+ Invokes inspiration and balance
+ Aligns to the pure joy and freedom that is our divine birthright
+ Connects you to the innocence and magic of the child within
+ Unlocks and circulates stagnant energy

Your personal experience with the crystal:

....

....

....

....

....

....

....

Stibnite

Crystal colour: Silver
Related chakras: Base, solar plexus and crown

Crystal meaning:
+ Supports your personal empowerment and transformation
+ Grounds your energy in the Earth so you feel supported
+ Assists you in dealing with fear of conflict and confrontation
+ Supports you to create healthy boundaries
+ Supports those who suffer from chronic anxiety
+ Enhances and supports the astral travel journey
+ Assists in dissolving apprehension and uncertainty

Your personal experience with the crystal:

....

....

....

....

....

....

....

Sugilite

Crystal colour: Various shades of purple, white and black
Related chakra: Heart

Crystal meaning:
+ Allows you to live in the present moment where you can receive all the gifts life has to offer
+ Strengthens your ability to walk your life path
+ Enhances devotion to your divine path and purpose
+ Enhances soul love and connection
+ Opens you to the divine truth and acceptance of your true mission on Earth

Your personal experience with the crystal:

....

....

....

....

....

....

....

Shungite

Crystal colour: Black
Related chakra: Base

Crystal meaning:

+ Allows you to deeply connect with your shadow side and receive the gifts it has to offer
+ Brings balance
+ Grounds and protects
+ Supports deep self-reflection
+ Assists in addressing and releasing painful, deep-seated negative behavioural patterns and cycles

Your personal experience with the crystal:

....

....

....

....

....

....

....

Sunstone

Crystal colour:
Various shades of
creams and orange
with tiny vibrant
speckles

Related chakra:
Solar plexus

Crystal meaning:

+ Connects to the energy of the divine source of all things, invoking great personal power in your life
+ Awakens self-empowerment, creating strength and courage
+ Enhances leadership qualities and the ability to listen to your higher guidance
+ Facilitates transformation
+ Releases blockages and resistance to change
+ Rekindles your passion for life
+ Assists in bringing in the light of the soul, helping one to move through depression

Your personal experience with the crystal:

....

....

....

....

....

....

....

Tanzanite

Crystal colour: Range of translucent to opaque purplish blues
Related chakra: Third eye

Crystal meaning:

✦ Opens you to your spiritual wisdom and sharing this knowledge from the heart
✦ Opens and activates the third eye chakra, enhancing clarity, vision and imagination
✦ Assists in communication with higher aspects of self, creating a deep knowing and wisdom in your life
✦ Supports you to make clear decisions in alignment with your soul purpose
✦ Allows you to see with clarity

Your personal experience with the crystal:

....

....

....

....

....

....

....

Tektite

Crystal colour: Black
Related chakra: Crown

Crystal meaning:

+ Enhances telepathic communication and intuitive gifts
+ Connects you with light beings from other planets and dimensions to receive knowledge, support and positive direction in life
+ Creates a strong protective energy shield around the aura
+ Facilitates the connection to aspects of yourself in other dimensions and planes of existence

Your personal experience with the crystal:

....

....

....

....

....

....

....

Tibetan Quartz

Crystal colour: Clear Quartz with black inclusions
Related chakras: All

Crystal meaning:
+ Holds all the properties of Clear Quartz
+ Resonates to the powerful energy of Tibet and it's deep wisdom
+ Allows you to find a place of peace and serenity and it's deep wisdom

Your personal experience with the crystal:

....

....

....

....

....

....

....

Tiger's Eye

Crystal colour: Varieties of browns, oranges, blacks and golds with reddish tinges
Related chakras: Sacral and solar plexus

Crystal meaning:

+ Allows you to see clearly into situations, making it a powerful crystal to assist in decision making
+ Allows you to open deeply to spiritual wisdom and live it on a day-to-day basis
+ Enhances courage and strength in your life
+ Allows you to stay focused on the task
+ Supports us in challenging and confrontational situations
+ Supports us in finding our inner truths and draws in the courage from our spirit to face our challenges

Your personal experience with the crystal:

....

....

....

....

....

....

....

Topaz

Crystal colour: Varied range of opaque to translucent colours, from clear to browns, greens, reds, whites, blues and yellows
Related chakras: All

Crystal meaning:

+ Powerful crystal to assist in manifestation and aligning to your higher purpose
+ Clears and cleanses the mind, creating clarity and a deeper sense of peace
+ Opens the crown chakra, bringing in the light of the cosmos for purification
+ Facilitates spiritual and creative expression
+ Calms and soothes the heart
+ Brings in a deeper gratitude and appreciation of our gifts

Your personal experience with the crystal:

....

....

....

....

....

....

....

Tourmaline — Black

Crystal colour: Black
Related chakra: Base

Crystal meaning:
+ Powerful grounding and protective crystal
+ Transmutes and dissolves any stuck or dormant energies in the body and auric field, creating a deep and powerful cleansing and purification
+ Strengthens and protects the aura, allowing you to feel safe in your own energy field
+ Assists in creating appropriate boundaries in your life
+ Powerful crystal to have around computers and telephones to dissolve unwanted electromagnetic energy
+ Unblocks and circulates stagnant energy

Your personal experience with the crystal:

....

....

....

....

....

....

....

Tourmaline — Dravite (Brown)

Crystal colour: Brown
Related chakras: Base and sacra

Crystal meaning:

+ Assists in healing past sexual issues, allowing you to move into a loving sexual union with your beloved
+ Activates and stimulates the base and sacral chakras, and assists in healing issues related to these chakras
+ Creates stability and grounding in your life, allowing you to feel safe and supported
+ Allows you to release any fear of change and move forward
+ Assists in releasing suppressed anger, frustration, sadness and disappointment

Your personal experience with the crystal:

....

....

....

....

....

....

....

Tourmaline — Green

Crystal colour: Opaque to translucent green
Related chakra: Heart

Crystal meaning:
+ Deep connection to the Earth and nature spirits
+ Opens you to receive the healing energy and wisdom held deep within the Earth
+ Purifies and strengthens the nervous system
+ Balances and harmonises the heart chakra, allowing for healing around any old wounds of the heart
+ Creates forgiveness and understanding
+ Sets you free from the restraints of fear
+ Encourages honouring of self and others

Your personal experience with the crystal:

....

....

....

....

....

....

....

Tourmaline — Indicolite (Blue)

Crystal colour: Opaque to translucent blue
Related chakras: Throat and third eye

Crystal meaning:

+ Deepens your intuition and psychic gifts
+ Assists in the communication and expression of true self from a deeper level of truth
+ Balances the mind and heart, allowing for a deeper space of inner peace
+ Allows you to move through shyness and more into your true essence

Your personal experience with the crystal:

....

....

....

....

....

....

....

Tourmaline — Pink

Crystal colour: Opaque to translucent pinks
Related chakras: Heart

Crystal meaning:

+ Stone of grace, aligning your soul to this sacred and divine vibration
+ Assists in releasing blame and guilt, allowing you to find a place of deep forgiveness
+ Powerfully opens and heals the heart, allowing you to come from a deeper place of unconditional love
+ Transforms any barriers or walls around the heart chakra, allowing you to open to the flow of giving and receiving
+ Opens you to experience the magic and joy that life has to share with us

Your personal experience with the crystal:

....

....

....

....

....

....

....

Tourmaline — Rubellite (Red)

Crystal colour: Opaque to translucent red
Related chakra: Sacral

Crystal meaning:

+ Enhances passion, strength and vitality
+ Awakens your inspiration and positive outlook and zest for life
+ Opens you to your passion and creativity
+ Good for teachers to keep the vibe and energy high in the room
+ Reignites the eternal flame within
+ Rejuvenates and restores energy
+ Revitalises the spirit
+ Releases worry and negative thinking

Your personal experience with the crystal:

....

....

....

....

....

....

....

Tourmaline — Watermelon

Crystal colour: Pink and green
Related chakras: Heart

Crystal meaning:

+ Stone of humility, aligning your soul to this powerful and divine vibration
+ Amplifies qualities of Green and Pink Tourmaline; the synergy of the pink and green crystals brings a powerful balancing and healing of the heart chakra, allowing you to love unconditionally
+ Opens and encourages you to experience the joy of life
+ Amplifies forgiveness and compassion on a global scale

Your personal experience with the crystal:

....

....

....

....

....

....

....

Tree root (petrified)

Crystal colour: Creams to dark browns
Related chakra: Base

Crystal meaning:

+ Deepens connection to our ancestors and their deep wisdom
+ Allows you to have your feet planted on the ground, creating balance and stability
+ Grounds and supports
+ Deepens connection to the ancient tree beings on the Earth and their healing energy

Your personal experience with the crystal:

....

....

....

....

....

....

....

Turquoise

Crystal colour: Turquoise
Related chakras: Heart
and throat

Crystal meaning:

+ Encourages you to listen from the heart
+ Deepens clarity and knowing of your true feelings and how
  to express them from a space of love
+ Opens you to feel, experience and express your own truth
+ Promotes honesty and integrity in your life
+ Opens the heart, allowing you to speak from a deep place
  of clarity and truth
+ Enhances self-expression

Your personal experience with the crystal:

....

....

....

....

....

....

....

Vivianite

Crystal colour: Dark green and blue
Related chakras: Heart and throat

Crystal meaning:

+ Powerfully transforms issues of the heart, allowing you to flow free in the essence of love
+ Awakens deep inspiration and success in your life
+ Connects to the joy and wonder of life

Your personal experience with the crystal:

....

....

....

....

....

....

....

Zincite

Crystal colour:
Variety of orange,
yellow and green
Related chakras: All

Crystal meaning:
+ Strengthens the bonds of family, tribe and community
+ Stimulates your creative flow
+ Deepens connection with the infinite possibilities of your life

Your personal experience with the crystal:

....

....

....

....

....

....

....

PART 3

Sharing in the wisdom and experiences
of others with the Crystal Kingdom

Case studies of crystal healing

Since I started my awakening with the Crystal Kingdom, I have had my own experiences, as well as hearing and sharing in many of the experiences of the students of the academy, and many other people's amazing, tangible and powerful experiences. Many of these experiences with the crystals have been incredibly potent and such a huge part of my transformation and healing, as well as that of many others. I know deeply in my heart that the Crystal Kingdom has loved, guided and assisted all of us along the way and know in my heart, without a doubt, the healing and magical essence of the Crystal Kingdom. Crystals truly are gifts from Mother Earth to assist us in our journey back to love and healing. Please allow me to share my own stories along with many other stories of how crystals have assisted in healing the mind, body and spirit.

First I would like to share a few of my own favourite stories of the magical Crystal Kingdom.

✦ ✦ ✦

I had a really bad fall down stairs in my home a few years ago. I was in shock and unable to move. My friend heard the noise and came running. She found me on my back on the floor at the bottom of the stairs. All I could say to her was 'Malachite and Hematite', so she got both crystals and laid them across my body. I lay on the floor for around 20 minutes and felt the crystals healing and supporting me. I had a miraculous recovery; the only bruise I had on me was on my little toe. I also had a strong message from the universe to slow down.

I was spending some sacred space with a beautiful crystal friend of mine. Often we had amazing experiences with crystals and I would love to share a very special experience with you. Jamie handed me a Tibetan Quartz Crystal. As I received this potent crystal in my hand I started to have a very intense reaction within and physically. My vision started to blur, and I could see the crystal energy vibrating and could feel it pulsating in my hand. In this powerful experience I started seeing little triangles appear on the face of the crystal. This lasted for about 20 seconds, then my vision returned to normal. I realised the triangles had stayed on the face of the crystal. Little ancient wisdom markings (record keepers) had manifested on the crystal and I was blessed to have witnessed it. I did know that crystals could do this; however, to see it and witness it with your own eyes is truly amazing. There are some things in life we just cannot prove and I feel this is the magic of these experiences; the mystery of the unknown.

Another amazing experience with Jamie happened in the same meeting where he introduced me to one of the special crystals he was working with, a Libyan Gold Tektite. I had never heard of this crystal before and fell in love with it. I deeply connected to this awesome crystal over the next few days and before Jamie left we decided we would infuse the energy of the crystal into a piece of beeswax that looked similar to the crystal. We placed an intention into the beeswax and out to the Crystal Kingdom that I would physically manifest myself a Libyan Gold Tektite Crystal.

The following week I attended a gem fest. I walked in the room where the gem fest was being held and there she was, waiting for me — a beautiful piece of Libyan Gold Tektite that looked exactly like the piece of beeswax Jamie and I had infused. Amazing!

One of the first experiences I ever had with a crystal was the first session I had with my teacher, Maggie. She was introducing each crystal to me and handed me an amazing Rock Ruby to connect with. I held this powerful crystal to my heart and I could feel its love and energy enter deeply inside. I started to cry and let go of lifetimes of trauma that I had held within my heart. Maggie insisted I take this beautiful crystal home with me so it could still work with me, and love and support me through my healing at this time. I put the crystal under my pillow to sleep with so I had it close to me.

The next morning I contemplated taking the crystal to work with me because I felt very soothed and held by its energy. However, I decided to leave the crystal at home because I did not want to risk losing it. I walked to the train station and caught the train to work, put my hand in my bag to reach for my book and guess what was in my bag? Yes, the crystal! At first I questioned myself and wondered if I had put the crystal in the bag, then realised that if I had put it in the bag I would have wrapped it in a cloth to ensure it was safe from getting scratched and broken. Then I realised the crystal must have put itself in the bag because I was quite sure that I had not. Crystals are energies and have an intelligence and consciousness of their own. They seem able to manifest themselves through space and time, depending on where they need to be for the healing of humanity. Incredible!

Many years ago I had an accident that left my jaw slightly out of alignment. The misalignment of my jaw caused a few problems with chewing and headaches. When I first discovered the amazing energy and healing properties of crystals I went through a stage of receiving many crystal healings from my teacher, Maggie. After a very deep and powerful crystal session with Maggie I sat up from the table and started to share with her what my experience was and my jaw clicked back into place. It was a little painful at first, then I realised my jaw had realigned itself. The next time I had an x-ray of my teeth I looked closely at the photo of my jaw and my jaw was straight again. I believe this had to do with several crystal healings over time, which assisted my physical body to align itself. Thank you Crystal Kingdom.

✦ ✦ ✦

Simonne Michelle-Wells, Melbourne, Victoria, Australia
I've had a fascination with crystals since I was a kid. Much to the amusement of my school friends I used to walk around with an amethyst in my bra when I was in high school. A few years ago I developed a

significant relationship with a crystal. I'd never had a real relationship with a crystal before, and it was this particular one that made me realise how wonderful and rewarding a deeply connected relationship with them can be.

I remember saying to my husband that I wasn't sure why, but I knew I needed a new Quartz Crystal. We went to the market and I chose a smallish one that gave me a beautiful, gentle vibration as I picked it up. Before long I felt driven to sleep with it in my (left) hand — something I've never done before. The amazing thing was that I would wake up every morning with it still in my hand.

I held that crystal all through the night for six weeks straight. Then, one morning, I woke up to find I wasn't holding it anymore. I fished it from the bed and knew that my crystal had done for me what it needed to do. I thanked it and gave it a well-deserved rest. I felt happy that I hadn't spent time wondering what the crystal was healing, I just trusted I was getting a healing on a deep level and that whatever it was about, it was all in Divine timing.

For a long time I'd actually been working on healing wounds connected with some of my core beliefs about sex and intimacy, and it was only after this six-week relationship with this crystal that I realised I'd finally come to a more grounded place within myself about these issues. I knew a deep healing had occurred. I was no longer filled with anxiety about 'fixing' my wounds, but rather, I'd come to a place of learning about acceptance and forgiveness instead. It marked a very significant change for me; one that has enabled me to move forward in a way I thought I never would.

I later found out from Rachelle that the crystal I was drawn to and had been holding through the night for those six weeks was a Goddess (Isis) Crystal; one of the Teacher (Master) Crystals. It helps us get in touch with our true essence and puts us in touch with the Goddess energy. It has powerful feminine energy, and is a powerful healing crystal for wounds of the heart.

I feel Divinely blessed for being drawn to this beautiful crystal that's had a profound effect on my life. I'm so happy I listened to my intuition and trusted my instincts about what to do with it. I have many, many crystals, but my Goddess (Isis) Crystal is deeply connected to my heart. She is a true friend.

✦ ✦ ✦

Siobhan Duncan, United Kingdom

I was called to do the foundation and intermediate courses after meeting Rachelle at Sydney's MBS (Mind Body Spirit) event in 2007. Crystals had always attracted me and I had a good collection so it was great to find a teacher who imparted the wisdom in such an authentic and far-reaching way. During the exercises it became evident that I had past life experience of healing using crystals, particularly with wands, and having completed the courses, I was drawn to experiment with making essences.

Following the instruction I learnt from Rachelle, I intuitively decided to make a combination essence for abundance. Having chosen the stones I wanted to use and meditating on their individual qualities, I embarked on making my first ever essence. Taking great care and intention, I created an essence under an auspicious eclipse moon. I gifted dosage bottles to my friends and asked them to report back to me, as well as taking it myself.

I must admit, I did overdose for the first couple of weeks; however, I felt I needed a great shift and that is exactly what I got. I was in an office job with a boss I really didn't like, where I wasn't appreciated and was really unhappy. Through taking the essence, I found the courage to confront and leave that job without knowing where I would go to next. Within days of resigning, I had an interview where I was hired instantly and found myself surrounded by excellent people in a great working environment which paid me a lot more and valued my skills. My lease was due to be renewed and I was bracing myself for a huge rent hike, which resulted in a $20 per week rise. A month later, I was gifted a large sum of money which assisted me in pursuing my dream of living overseas.

My friends reported that it was working for them as well. One friend who runs her own business was having problems with clients cancelling and was worried about meeting her premise's rent. I advised her and her husband to take the essence regularly. After taking one dosage on the Sunday, she had people booking in for a variety of services and wanting to return. Her husband finally received a compensation payout they thought he would never get and bought a new car at auction for an exceptionally low price compared to its value. Since taking the essence more regularly, she now has other practitioners who have approached her to work out of her premises a few days a week, alleviating her financial worries of meeting the rent and allowing her more time with her child.

The learning I take from this is that, through being creative and using your intuition and intention, the crystals will respond and guide you to what you need. I have just created a new variation of the essence and I'm looking forward to hearing how my friends experience this, and to learn the subtle difference between the new version and the original.

✦ ✦ ✦

Lexis Trinidad, Perth, Western Australia, Australia

I was inspired to create a beautiful fairy garden full of love, light and crystals. I wanted to honour all of the beautiful nature beings that we share space with, a safe sacred space for them all to enjoy. I started by placing river stones in a small circle, then placed different crystals such as Apophyllite, Selenite, Celestial Quartz, Singing Quartz, Ocean Jasper and Green Apophyllite. I created a ceremony, starting with calling in all of the directions, asking Mother Earth and Great Spirit for their support in creating a sacred space. By the time I had finished calling in the directions, a crow's feather had appeared in the north of the garden. So I blessed the crow and placed the feather in the north of the circle of stones. Then, as I walked around the garden area I found another three beautiful feathers, all black and white. I then placed these in all of the other directions of the garden. What a wonderful blessing, so I left the garden content that there was a safe space where all of the Earth beings could play.

About a week later we had one of our first rains for the winter and I went to the garden to honour the beings and share love with them. As I looked at the garden I found something shining in the sand. As I pulled it out of the sand I had tingles all over as I realised it was a small crystal skull about 1.5 inches in diameter, made out of Smoky Quartz. It was beautiful and had rainbows all of the way through it. Some of the back of the skull was missing. A few days later the back of the skull appeared too. After meditating with the skull it was placed back in the garden for all of the nature beings to enjoy. Such a wonderful gift and acknowledgement from our nature beings to find the crystal skull. Later I had discovered that a friend who lived there before me had lost the skull about a year ago. What a wonderful experience.

✦ ✦ ✦

Suzanne Tennison, Sunshine Coast, Queensland, Australia

This was a profound healing I experienced in one of the workshops I attended at The Academy of Crystal Awakening. It was the final day of the workshop. I lay on the massage table with crystals placed on my heart and throat chakras as well as a layout of crystals placed on my heart in a design for an inner child experience. The other participant stood beside me, sensing my vulnerability, comforting me at every moment.

I was guided in meditation gently to meet my inner child, the aspect of me that has been forgotten and lost over time, the innocence of my childhood. She was sad and I realised it was time for her to be happy again. I was guided to take her to a special sacred place, so we went to the beach and played and walked along the sand. I then realised that I did not have my inner child with me. The inner child seemed to be outside my being. So I placed her on my heart and put my crystal wand there too and held her tightly. Rachelle, the facilitator/instructor came over and held my right side. The pure bliss, sensation and profound experience of my inner child being placed back in my heart was unbelievable. I feel this happened because I worked from the heart and connected into the crystals. Trust is the big thing for my inner child. I have regained trust and safety.

After the workshop, I kept saying the word safety, which embraced the healing.

For the next day and a half, my body was in a state of bliss, my heart pulsing strongly and full of love. I felt very uplifted as I became aware of a major distinction between my previous existence and how I felt now. I seemed like a different person who has transformed through love, and now my spirit is alive and pulsating.

✦ ✦ ✦

Nina Climpson, Sydney, New South Wales, Australia

I was at some markets one day with a friend who is not interested in crystals at all. I bought a Prehnite Crystal at a stall, then we went to a cafe for a coffee. While there I took out my new baby and my friend asked to look at it. Within a couple of minutes she began to talk about a phobia she had and was finally doing something about. As she talked she became quite emotional and began to cry, then said she didn't know what was wrong with her. I told her how proud she should be as this was a big thing she had done to tackle this phobia after so many years. All this time she had been holding the Prehnite Crystal (good for phobias), then suddenly said how nice it felt and handed it back to me. I said that it had done its job, but it went right over her head.

✦ ✦ ✦

Donna Davis, Singleton, New South Wales, Australia

I had an allergy in my left arm from a horse bite and had it for some years. I had tests, scans, X-rays and an MRI done on it and they showed nothing was wrong. At times I could not even use my arm, and when I wanted to lift it I would sometimes have to use my right hand to support it.

One day I purchased a crystal Black Tourmaline bracelet and placed it around my left wrist and within a short time it started to hurt. I thought I should remove it; however felt a strong intuition to leave it on to see what would happen. After about three days I continued to wear it by day only. Not sure how long after, however I realised that the swelling had gone down and there was no soreness. I just couldn't believe that these amazing crystals could do such a thing, as doctors had told me there was nothing wrong. Amazing!

I also had another recent experience with a Rose Quartz with a hint of dark purple in it. I have had a lot of tingling in my left hand due to the work I have been doing. I was drawn to this crystal very strongly, and after purchasing this crystal I was then compelled to hold it in my left hand, only to feel a strong sensation of drawing in my hand. I held it on and off for some time, as I was driving at the time, and again to my surprise (confirmation) the crystal had gone to work and taken the numbness away. I work in a cold area with my hands so this numbness was due to extreme cold temperatures which had left my fingers with something like frostbite on the ends of them.

I love my crystals and could not live without them. I also help others to find all kinds of strength from crystals for whatever situation they are going through.

✦ ✦ ✦

Angela, Brisbane, Queensland, Australia

Just over a year ago I spotted a small Clear Quartz crystal in a shop in Adelaide. It was about 40 cm long and I was especially drawn to the formation inside the crystal There were what appeared to be five rocky steps leading upward and it reminded me of life and the rocky roads we sometimes encounter on our journey to our ultimate goals. I called it 'Stairway to Heaven', and on taking it back to my home in Brisbane I placed it on top of one of my stereo speakers.

Two weeks later I chose this crystal, along with four others, to take with me on my spiritual journey in Egypt. These crystals were all wrapped in two silk scarves and then placed in a small drawstring bag in my day bag, so that I could bring them out to 'breathe' whenever possible.

And so our journey through Egypt began, with daily meditations within various ancient temples, including a dawn meditation between the paws of the Sphinx. Each time we had a meditation I would bring my crystals out of their bag and lay them on the ground beside me on top of the scrunched up silk, so that they too could enjoy the truly spiritual experience within each ancient site.

On the fourth day of our journey we boarded our bus at am, headed along the Nile and out into the desert, to the Step Pyramid of King Zoser at Saqqarra. One by one we entered the tomb of this ancient pharaoh by sparse torchlight and made ourselves comfortable on the somewhat bumpy floor. And once again I brought my crystals out and laid them down on the ground beside me.

By the end of this particular meditation I was feeling quite agitated, so without pause I literally dumped everything that I had laid beside me back into my day pack and headed for the exit. Outside it was just breaking dawn and the fresh air helped my 'mood' somewhat. I didn't return to the tomb to take photos, opting just to enjoy the break of day and the total silence that only the desert offers.

Back in our motel room later in the day, I was sorting through my bag and, to my horror, realised that my little crystal was nowhere to be found. I knew I had it in the tomb, but had no recall of putting it back in my bag. I searched again and again over the next few days and even dismantled my over-bulging suitcase in the hope that it would be somewhere in my possession. I finally had to accept that maybe it hadn't wanted to leave Egypt.

Two and half weeks later, after a wonderful trip, I returned home late at night and unceremoniously dumped everything on the lounge room floor, hit the shower and then bed. On awakening the next morning, I wandered half asleep up the hallway and stopped dead in my tracks. For there, on my stereo speaker, was my 'Stairway to Heaven' crystal, exactly where it had sat for the two weeks prior to the trip. Immediately

I questioned my sanity, but quickly dismissed any doubts that I had about the sequence of events that had occurred.

Several days after my return I had my photos developed, and there was a photo I had taken in the tomb of another girl. The photo was taken in complete darkness, but along her left side was a long white light, similar to a firefly in flight, running the entire length of the photo, from top to bottom. Was this my crystal 'taking flight'?

A month ago I flew again to Adelaide for eight days of courses and again packed my little crystal, along with the other four that had also been to Egypt. Each day at the commencement of our course, I would place those same five crystals on their silk under my chair. And again, after four days of classes, my little crystal was nowhere to be found. That evening, another rigorous search of my day pack, my car and my suitcase revealed nothing . . . a waste of time searching really because I knew I had put it under the chair that morning.

I was starting to wonder if maybe I was responsible for all these disappearances, maybe I was subconsciously hiding it or something. If what happened in Egypt wasn't 'bizarre' enough, here I was searching for it again. But I am one of the most organised people I know, 'a place for everything and everything in its place' type of girl, and I KNEW that it had just disappeared, again! Five days later, after a thorough repack of all my bags on the eve prior to flying home, there was still no sign of it anywhere.

So naturally, as soon as I walked in my front door, I looked to the stereo speaker, expecting by now to see it sitting there. But alas, it wasn't and I resigned myself to the fact that it had finally found itself a new home somewhere in Adelaide. It was never really mine to keep, I figured.

And that was that, I thought, until I unpacked my bags . . . and there it was, in the bottom of my day pack! This time I didn't even question myself, I just accepted that the guardian of the crystal had its own agenda.

So what happens next? Will I take it away with me again? A part of me is intrigued to know what will happen if I do; but the other part of me thinks that I shouldn't mess with nature, and if it doesn't want to go, then I should just let it be. The formations inside the crystal have changed and it looks less and less like a stairway. Maybe I should change its name?

✦ ✦ ✦

Jackie Thornton, Canberra, Australian Capital Territory, Australia

I was first introduced to crystals when I was going through a very rough time in my life. I was suffering from very crippling panic attacks and a friend of mine gave me some crystals that she thought might help. I was very sceptical about the entire process, but figured I would give crystals a genuine chance. During my next panic attack I reached for some Sodalite and Hematite. I held them and placed them on parts of my body that were feeling the physical effects of the attack. While they didn't stop the panic attack, they certainly made it a lot easier to get through it, so much so that I became absolutely fascinated by crystals and their beautiful and powerful energy.

Wanting to learn more, I found myself doing more and more research. A friend of mine told me about Crystal Awakening's workshops and I jumped at the chance. Each workshop was an amazing experience. It taught me a lot about myself, my strengths and my weaknesses, and that scientifically crystals are used in everyday appliances, etc., but mainly that I can help others with the help of our beautiful crystals. I am now a certified crystal healer and I now have my own business selling crystals, a very proud moment for me. Without the help of crystals and Crystal Awakening I would not have been able to achieve this milestone in my life.

✦ ✦ ✦

Marnie Chattaway, Mandurah, Western Australia, Australia

I had been going through some family issues about four or five years ago. There was a lot of stress around my side of the family and I wanted to release it and feel better. I'd also felt a huge build-up of energy within myself, and knowing that some of it wasn't mine, I decided I would try some assistance from the crystals. I usually go with my intuition when choosing one, and I wanted something to jump out at me in relation to clearing myself of this energy. Unfortunately, in my collection there wasn't one that appealed, so I took myself off to my local crystal shop.

A beautiful piece of tumbled Charoite jumped out at me as soon as I walked in the door so that's exactly what I needed. Once home, I cleansed it gently over white sage incense and that night I placed it inside my pillowcase, under my pillow, in the hope that it would help me find restful sleep and I could let go of my worries. My hubby went to night shift that night, and after putting my children to bed I happily settled down to sleep myself. I had been exhausted after restless sleep the week previous and constant abstract dreams. By the time I had fallen into bed I'd completely forgotten that my piece of Charoite was there.

About four hours into my sleep, I suddenly awoke. I was lying flat on my back, almost rigid, and an incredible heat coming from my left hand. When I woke fully and understood my surroundings, I realised I had the piece of Charoite in my left hand and was clutching it tightly! I was astounded that it was there, considering it had been tucked safely in my pillowslip under my pillow hours before I'd gone to sleep and even forgotten it was there! The heat and energy emanating from the gem was just amazing, and I felt immediately calm. I took a deep breath and released my stranglehold on it and placed it gently on my bedside table. As I slipped back into slumber I remembered that I'd had a dreamless sleep before I woke at that point, and I felt amazingly at peace.

The rest of the night went without incident and when I woke in the morning I felt like I'd slept for about three days. My piece of Charoite was still by my bed, and my head felt amazingly clear. I felt as if something had detached — of what I wasn't sure at the time — and even though my family issues continued after that night I was able to disconnect to some point without it draining me completely. I still have my beautiful piece of Charoite to this day. I never underestimate the power of crystals and recommend them to everyone!

✦ ✦ ✦

Tracy Brumby-Cameron, Kangaroo Point, Brisbane, Queensland, Australia

I attended my Crystal Awakening intensive workshop and was excited and intrigued about what was possible. I decided that I would make some crystal essences as I thought it would be a great way to help people heal with crystals, both outside and inside of the body.

My ritual started many days before the last day of the waxing of the full moon with planning what I wanted to do, what my intention for my essences would be, what materials I would need, where I would do it. With all those plans in place, on the night before the full moon I commenced my creative process to create my healing chakra essences. It was a beautiful and powerful experience. I called in all the ascended healers to assist me in making my healing chakra essences.

As soon as I put the crystals in the jars inside the purified water the energy began to generate. I was so excited. I placed a grid around my essences using my Goddess (Isis) Crystal as the centre of the grid.

Over the three nights of the waxing of the moon, the full moon and the waning of the full moon, my crystal essences were done. As I made the mother essences I felt a sense of giving birth to a part of me as well as something bigger than me, universal healing.

Some of my success stories have included clearing diarrhoea, stomach cramps and headaches within 10 minutes of taking the essence. I personally used to suffer terribly from mosquito bites that would welt up for a month. I dosed up on my heart chakra essence made from Rose Quartz and the bites were gone in three days. I was astonished and excited; this really works.

I now take a dose of the combined chakra essences daily and I feel great.

✦ ✦ ✦

Denise Parker, Victoria Park, Brisbane, Queensland, Australia

My 12-year-old son came home from school with an extremely high temperature. He was sitting on my bed feeling very dizzy and ill. It felt like he was coming down with an aggressive flu.

He lay on the bed really struggling and I felt drawn to give him a large black Obsidian Crystal sphere the size of a small bowling ball. He wrapped his arms around it, drew it into his chest and fell asleep within a few minutes.

When he woke his eyes were clear, the temperature gone, and he was energised, bright and happy. It was amazing to see the transformation that took place within an hour. There is no doubt in my mind that this amazing crystal had a profound healing effect on him.

✦ ✦ ✦

Sky Anderson, Uki, New South Wales, Australia

My seven-year-old son had been having sleepless nights for the past 12 months. He was seeing spirits in his room and becoming quite fearful. I was running out of ideas as to what to try next, when we were in a crystal shop and he was drawn to the Kyanite Crystals. He said he needed them and chose four large pieces.

When we got home I asked him why he chose them and he said they were going to help him, but didn't elaborate.

That evening at bedtime he seemed calmer and showed me where he had put the crystals — they were in the corners of the room creating some kind of crystal grid. From that night on he was able to sleep and said the crystals made him feel safe. Thank you, Kyanite.

✦ ✦ ✦

Jodie, Sydney, New South Wales, Australia

I had just finished uni, completing a Fine Arts/Teaching degree, and begun teaching casually. I was lost and confused. My art course had gotten me nowhere and teaching in mainstream high schools was a really unrewarding experience for me. I felt that I was always having to hide my true nature to fit in. I knew there and then that I was not doing what I was meant to do.

I have always had an interest in crystals. I used to dig for them in my backyard as a child and quite often received them as gifts. I would buy them quite regularly as I got older and keep them close, but it wasn't until I sat in on one of Rachelle's seminars about crystals that I realised their wonderful qualities. Rachelle discussed a lot of crystals, but the one which particularly stood out for me was the Awakening Crystal (Elestial). I thought to myself, this is my crystal, I have to have one of these! It was like it called out to me. I spent days looking for one of these crystals and finally found one in a crystal store in Picton. I couldn't stop looking at it and could feel a sort of heat coming from it. Over the next few days I began working with it and programmed it to help me find my life's purpose. Not long after, one morning I woke up to get the newspaper and look for a new job (I have never bought a newspaper in my life). I looked through and saw this perfect job staring me in the face, teaching autistic children in a specialised school. Even though I had relatively little experience teaching autistic children, I applied. I had always felt a strong connection with them. Shortly after I got a phone call from the school asking me to come in for an interview and not long after I got the job. I have now been teaching there for just under a year and I love it, and feel that I have made a lot of progress with the kids I have taught. Also, when I wear crystal pendants to work, all of the kids are fascinated with them and come up and touch them. I feel that I am at the beginning of this journey and that so many great things are going to unfold. This experience has made me realise how much crystals can help us to live our life purpose and to love life.

✦ ✦ ✦

ACCREDITED TEACHERS OF THE ACADEMY OF CRYSTAL AWAKENING

The Crystal Kingdom put out a calling to passionate souls who would like to teach and share in the love and wisdom of their Kingdom. This calling was heard by a select few, the amazing new wave of teachers who have trained through The Academy of Crystal Awakening.

I feel deeply honoured and blessed to introduce you to these amazing teachers who will now be facilitating the Academy's popular life transforming and highly sought after Crystal Awakening foundation and intermediate workshops in Australia.

Rachelle invites you to have your own experience with her dynamic and passionate accredited teachers of the Academy, as you allow the crystals and Mother Earth to amplify your essence and lead you on a journey of self-discovery and love. Crystals, the healing energies of Mother Earth, amplify and bring more love and light into our consciousness, enabling and supporting us in healing and transformation as we rediscover our pure, natural state of being; all loving, all knowing, all wise as we connect deeply with ourselves, each other and All That Is.

Each teacher is accredited by the Academy and the National Healers Federation in Brisbane, and has been personally trained by Rachelle, the founder and principal of the Academy. Our powerful and dedicated fully accredited teachers are located Australia-wide. Please contact our teachers directly with your enquiries and bookings.

We invite you to visit the teacher section on the Academy's website, www.crystalawakening.com/teachers.html, for workshop dates and more information on accredited teachers in your area.

I now invite you to share in some of the teachers' stories of how the Crystal Kingdom has assisted them in their transformation, and guided and supported them on their healing journey.

✦ ✦ ✦

Lisa Cincotta, Melbourne, Victoria, Australia
Divine Harmony
lisac.divineharmony@gmail.com
www.divineharmony.com.au

My crystal experience started many years ago, at a time in my life where I was searching for love and support. I was going through depression and I was a single mum when the Crystal Kingdom started calling on me to connect with them to find inner love, peace and wisdom. I started by making crystal elixirs, creating crystal grids and using tumbled crystals. I would invoke their energy to assist me when I was feeling down, confused and unwell, receiving the love they projected to me, allowing me to feel the love I had deep inside. I introduced crystals to my son at a young age, and we called on them to assist our pets' passing, in particular his budgie (they were like best friends). It helped my son, as a nine year old, to know the crystals assisted his budgie on his new journey. In 2008, my mum was diagnosed with a rare small cell carcinoma, an aggressive tumour in her lung. I facilitated some crystal healings during her treatment, and she believes that the crystals assisted her in surviving and being in a better physical state than otherwise expected by the specialists.

On a personal level, after these and many other profound healings, I had a calling to learn more about the Crystal Kingdom. In 2009, I became aware of Rachelle Charman, of The Academy of Crystal Awakening, who was facilitating crystal workshops, 'Crystal Foundation' and 'Crystal Intermediate'.

Wow, I thought I had a strong connection with crystals until Rachelle took us on a deeper journey. It was like being on a crystal high, now that I had received a deeper experience with the Crystal Kingdom. The information Rachelle shared with us in her crystal workshops was a beautiful experience. She took us on journeys that I had never experienced before. Rachelle's love and knowledge allowed me to understand crystals and how they can assist us in many ways. After her workshop I enjoyed working with crystals even more. I started hearing them clearer and for the first time in my life I could start removing the layers of baggage that I had spent many years carrying. It was easier with the help of the crystals, without fear, as they assisted me to step into my power.

In 2010 I attended Rachelle Charman's next workshop, the 'Advanced Earth Wisdom Shamanic Workshop', as I am very drawn to the shamanic ways of living. Once again I deepened my connection with more crystals, and many different shifts and layers were removed. We all have many journeys and challenges in our lives; all we need is to call on the assistance of our crystal friends and their Devas, the most sacred gifts from Mother Earth.

In the last two years I have become more centred and more in touch with my own essence. I believe the crystals, with their organic love and support, have assisted me on my journey when I have felt lost.

✦ ✦ ✦

Phet Capizzi, Adelaide, South Australia, Australia
Crystal and Reiki Academy
phethealing@gmail.com
www.healingwellness.org

In 2007–08, during the world financial crisis which caused many businesses to fall, I was very sick with my skin full of blisters and rashes. Some doctors said it was from the stress of running my business, others said it was due to pollutions, and others even said it was from old age. Many friends and professionals believed I hade contracted AIDS, HIV or hepatitis. Over time I had my skin removed and scraped for a laboratory test to see what was going on. I was also on numerous antibiotics, allergy tablets, creams, antiseptics and anything else you can think of. No-one knew what was wrong with me! The doctors had me on saline drips as they did not know what to do with me. I thought I was dying. Each time my blood pressure went up the doctors gave me stronger medicines and I would get constant itching. My face was full of rashes and blisters, and I had cold sores over my mouth, eyes, chin, arms, palms and fingers. I looked like a 70-year-old woman.

After filing for bankruptcy in 2008, I lost my home, my cars, my friends, my family (including my children), my three pharmacies, my super fund and my savings. I cried and screamed and hit rock bottom in my life. I went through what people call the dark night of the soul. I then decided to turn my life to New Age, in search of answers to my life, my illness and of course the answers to 'why me?'

While I was travelling a lady handed me a book written by Doreen Virtue called Healing with the Angel. I read the book on the way back from the USA and was introduced to Rose Quartz and Amethyst crystals. I then ask my friend to find these crystals as we were curious to see what they looked like. At the time I had no knowledge of crystals, besides diamond rings. I then went on to attend various healing workshops and learnt the wisdom of energetic healing. In late 2009 while holding a Goddess (Isis) Crystal during the meditation in the Isis Lotus healing workshop, I received the message from Isis that my illness was due to the interaction between my blood pressure tablets and alcohol, which I do drink regularly while having dinner at night. I was stunned by this information as no-one would expect this information, especially me, as I am a pharmacist!

I went to see the doctor the very next day and told him. My tablets were changed and half of my body healed within six weeks. I continued to seek specialist advice and continued to learn to avoid food and drinks that contain sulphites, sulphur and MSG, including breakfast cereal and dried fruits. The Goddess (Isis) Crystal hence became my daily companion, and I have learned to have more compassion and forgive myself and others for all the sad events that happened in the last 15 years and in my past.

I send much love and give thanks to all of the people who were part of my life journey. They are my support and the backbone of who I have become today: well, happy and healthy. I give thanks to all my masters and the Crystal Kingdom for giving me new sight in a new light and direction.

✦ ✦ ✦

Lyndall Rumenos, Dunsborough, Western Australia, Australia
Sacred Harmony
info@sacredharmony.com.au
www.sacredharmony.com.au

As soon as I laid eyes on her I knew she was mine. She was of medium size, clothed in the colours of pale blue and soft tan, rough and unpolished, but to me she emanated beauty. And so that day in September 2010 I bought 'Miss Blue Lace Agate' — I knew she would look perfect in my healing room.

Towards the end of October 2010 I attended Rachelle's Crystal Awakening intensive and advanced workshops. I was delighted to read in Rachelle's Crystals for Healing guide that Blue Lace Agate can be used for thyroid conditions. It became obvious to me, because of my thyroid challenge (Hashimoto's Disease), that my Blue Lace Agate Crystal would have to change rooms. On arriving in my bedroom she beckoned to be placed on my bedside cabinet, where she has dutifully remained since. Silently and without fuss, she worked her evening magic. A routine blood test a few months later revealed all was well, no need to adjust my oroxine medication. Previous to this, and for various reasons, my thyroid levels had been erratic.

✦ ✦ ✦

Andara, Sydney, New South Wales, Australia
Life Path Energies
lifepathenergies@hotmail.com
www.lifepathenergies.com

It was a beautiful sunny day and I was preparing for meditation. I took my Amethyst and Rose Quartz hearts into my right hand, which I closed. Lying down, relaxing and going deeper and deeper with each breath, I started my past life meditation journey. As the soft music was playing I found myself in the green lush place of the land of Avalon. The mist was slowly lifting from the lake. I turned around and I saw a man standing behind me, looking at me with love, and I knew I had come home. I took his hand into mine and walked away.

It was time to come back. Slowly opening my eyes, I become aware of my surroundings. Suddenly I felt panic. I did not feel my crystals in my hand anymore — it was empty. I started to shake and told my friends, 'my crystals are missing', so we all started to look for them. After almost giving up I picked up my Avalon pouch that I had on the chair and they were inside. Now how they got there I do not know. I was lying down the whole time, not moving, and the pouch was at least seven feet away. For me it was another miracle, experiencing the magic of crystals teleporting and telling me that what happened in my meditation was real.

Crystals carry far more knowledge and wisdom than was once thought, and we are only just starting to recognise this. But they are waiting and willing us to learn from them, even time travelling.

✦ ✦ ✦

Carol Graham, Sunshine Coast, Queensland, Australia
Carmic Crystals
carmic.crystals@hotmail.com

I was feeling very sad and lonely in my life as over time I had lost a lot of people who were very close to me. I realised I was not allowing myself to get too close to anyone in fear of losing them again, so I started working with the beautiful crystal Hiddenite. I had been connecting with this crystal for three or four days when I felt my heart open up and so much sadness release, and I cried until I could not cry anymore. I was lucky to have very supportive people around me at the time. I feel as if my heart has opened up again and I feel so much love come into my heart. I am truly thankful to the wonderful crystal Hiddenite for helping me open my heart again and look forward to my next experience.

✦ ✦ ✦

Kerry Marsh, Brisbane, Queensland, Australia
Crystal Discoveries
kerry@crystaldiscoveries.com.au
www.crystaldiscoveries.com.au

I share my passion for crystal healings with both people and animals, and have witnessed the amazing healing power of crystals first hand. None as dramatic as with my Labrador, Ebony.

She was seven years old when she tore her cruciate ligament. She underwent surgery and had an artificial ligament inserted. Following the surgery she experienced immense pain in the back right leg. In order to reduce the pain she was experiencing, as well as stimulate bone and ligament growth, I used a combination of crystals including Malachite, Hematite and Tiger's Eye in conjunction with traditional veterinarian prescribed medication.

The crystals aided her recovery significantly as her limping and swelling was greatly reduced, more than it might have otherwise been. Weather changes cause ongoing aggravation to this leg, and I regularly maintain treatment for pain and arthritis with a regime of various crystals. During post-operative recovery, a combination of anxiety and confinement left her with chronic cystitis and continual bladder infections. A range of antibiotics temporarily cleared the problem, only to find the infections would recur after a number of weeks, and sometimes within a few days.

The situation was quite serious, resulting in a complete shutdown of her bladder and complete loss of bladder control. Her condition was so severe that her annual vaccination was postponed due to a shortened life expectancy. A crystal combination of Prehnite and Golden Labradorite aided in the eventual recovery from these ongoing inflammations, in conjunction with prescribed veterinarian medications.

Recovery went so well that she was able to have her vaccination within a few months of treatment.

✦ ✦ ✦

Bobbie Powe, Mandurah, Western Australia, Australia
Arania's Light
araniaslight@hotmail.com

My personal experience with crystals has been quite profound over the years, but the one that has had the most impact on my life is the Awakening Smoky Quartz (Elestial). This special crystal, which is about the size of my hand, has many key markings and a very large ancient wisdom marking on the surface. I feel it has helped me transform over the last four years and deal with many life lessons. I meditate and hold it quite often as it supports and gives me comfort on an emotional level. Every time I have had some major change or an extreme life lesson, this amazing crystal has helped me, especially when my Nan and sister passed away. I would connect in with my crystal and hold it for comfort and started to realise that its shape would change. It is like every time I learn or experience something important, part of the crystal disappears. I fully believe this crystal holds messages and lessons for me, and as I learn these lessons, it changes shape to reveal a new one. This powerful Awakening (Elestial) Crystal has brought me lots of comfort and peace, and also understanding about my journey here in this lifetime.

✦ ✦ ✦

Rebecca Privilege, Perth, Western Australia, Australia
mail@naturalhealingtherapies.com.au
Natural Healing Therapies Australia

Whilst I've had many wonderful experiences with the Crystal Kingdom, my most profound has been with a Clear Quartz laser wand. Why? It was with this crystal that I started my journey into the wonderful world of psychic surgery.

The wand becomes an extension of my hands; it's used to working with me in this way and retains its innate wisdom as we work together.

I have used this wand to work on endometriosis, clearing away 'old' cells in the uterus from a termination of miscarriage to allow wonderful new cells to grow with a new pregnancy, and working with nerves to alleviate headaches and migraines, old fractures, new fractures and anything else we feel we need to work on.

This wand stays and works with me to this day.

✦ ✦ ✦

Jessica Dao, Adelaide, South Australia, Australia
The Pyramid of Light
info@thepyramidoflight.com
www.thepyramidoflight.com

At the Crystal Awakening foundation workshop, we all got to learn how to set up crystal grids. They are amazing and powerful energy magnifying tools. After my workshop with Rachelle, I got home and set up a grid in my living room. In the centre of the grid is a large Clear Quartz Crystal with two smaller crystals attached to it. This crystal is about 25 centimetres tall. I felt the powerful energy immediately after the grid was activated. I then went and picked up my two children from school, Jesse who was then 14 years of age and Joshua, 10. Jesse is an Indigo child and Josh is a Crystal. When we got home, Jesse walked into the living room and he didn't notice anything, but Josh immediately said 'Mum, I feel very tingles in this room!' After a while Josh got used to the tingle feeling. I told both the children about the grid. Jesse said he didn't feel anything and he didn't like it because he doesn't believe in it. I told them not to move the crystal otherwise the grid would be inactivated.

One day I went out and came home, noticing the energy had dropped. I immediately asked the children if they had moved the crystals. Jesse said, 'How the hell do you know that?' He started to wonder about the grid so he shifted the crystal again on purpose on another occasion and I immediately noticed and told him off. Now Jesse leaves my grid alone!

Another beautiful story happened with my favourite moonstone ring, which I bought from Dubai a few years ago. It's the symbol of purity and peace of mind and heart for me. After the Crystal Awakening teacher training retreat, I decided to give this ring to one of the teachers in training. As I put the ring on her finger, I said to her, 'This is a symbol of receiving love, each time you look at this ring you will see my face and it will remind you that you need to receive as well as give love'. A face manifested in front of our eyes. It's such a beautiful and pure face on the ring.

✦ ✦ ✦

Denise Gee, Sydney, New South Wales, Australia
Guidance of Light
www.guidanceoflight.com
info@guidanceoflight.com

In June 2010 I was in Queensland for a workshop and stopped in to visit friends who lived in Brisbane. During my stay my friend mentioned a crystal shop that she knew I would love, so she drove me there before taking me to the airport for my trip home to Sydney. The crystal shop was located in Brisbane's West End and was called Crystal Earth, and what an exquisite shop it was. When I stepped into the shop I noticed all the large crystals sitting on the floor, the smaller crystals were crammed on the bookshelves and table tops, there were pagan items, spells, pendants, books: a crystal lover's delight, that's for sure. As I made my way around the shop, I found myself standing in front of the round table which was in the middle of the room. I reached out to one particular crystal and when I picked it up in my hand the crystal heated up immediately. I could feel it connecting to me as its energy pulsated in my hand. The card at the front read 'Yellow Opal: The Letting Go Crystal'. I knew immediately that I was to take this crystal home with me.

At the time, I was preparing to cut ties to a friendship that had run its course. Many other friends had commented that this person's energy was not quite right and it wasn't until an incident at a cafe that this person's behaviour towards me changed and I got to see their real self. Working with this crystal assisted me to hear my inner guidance, which suggested I step away from this friendship and move on. The Yellow Opal works with the stomach area, especially with gut instincts. It helps you to stand your ground on issues you feel deeply about. It also releases from your mind, body and spirit, negative emotions and bitterness. My experience with working with the Yellow Opal allowed me to go deep within and go to a place I had never been before. It allowed the issues of this friendship to gently come to the surface. I was ready to let this friendship go and move on, and working with this crystal helped me to stand my ground and do what was best for me.

✦ ✦ ✦

Kahu Martin, Sydney, New South Wales, Australia
KahMar Healing
www.kahmarhealing.com
info@kahmarhealing.com

I want to share my experience about crystal grids and the energy that can be amplified in order to manifest your worldly desires. I have always believed in positive affirmations and setting your intention in order to achieve what you want.

Shortly after completing the foundation workshop with Rachelle Charman, I was immediately attracted to the crystal grid in order to manifest my dreams and goals with the use of a vision board. I started working on my board by adding pictures, words and symbols in order to manifest what I wanted most at the present moment.

I completed my vision board with pictures of a holiday to America to go to Disneyland, and a new car. I bought a Quartz 'Generator' Crystal for the centre of my crystal grid to amplify the energy out into the universe. The larger the crystal, the more energy the crystal will amplify. The grid consisted of six Clear Quartz terminator points in order to create the six-pointed star. I placed other crystals in my grid, such as Hematite for grounding the energy into reality, Rose Quartz for love and appreciation to the universe for manifesting my desires, Citrine Crystals to create abundance, and Amethyst Crystals for protection. The grid was programmed to store the intention in order to make it a powerful manifestation tool.

I created a sacred space for my grid and activated it by saying a positive incantation while spiralling the energy out into the cosmos. Whenever I had a feeling I would add more crystals to the grid in order to create a mandela. This just made the energy of the grid more intense and I could really feel the energy emanating from it. Within days things just began to fall into place. Plans began to happen and finances just seemed to appear in order for me to make my dreams a reality. Since working with crystal grids with the help of vision boards, I have been able to manifest things that I never thought possible.

✦ ✦ ✦

Marcel Hutton, Sydney, New South Wales, Australia
KahMar Healing
www.kahmarhealing.com
info@kahmarhealing.com

I have suffered many years from an excruciating stomach complaint. I participated in The Academy of Crystal Awakening's intermediate workshop with Rachelle Charman (founder of The Academy of Crystal

Awakening) in June 2010. As part of learning we connected with the Master Crystals and were asked to choose one to meditate with. I was immediately drawn to the Time Travel (Time Link) Crystal, with a bridge that connects your soul with the past. This crystal is recognisable by the two parallel lines spiralling to the left that create a rhomboidal shape along one of the faces looking like a small window. I deeply connected with the energy of the crystal and closed my eyes, focusing on my soul star, and just let my body travel to the destination of its choice.

I was immediately taken back to a time when I was in a very old hospital that looked like it had very limited medical supplies or sterile conditions. My legs were in stirrups and I had immense pain from going through childbirth. I endured the pain but felt myself getting weaker. There was so much blood from what I believe to be a haemorrhage and complications with the birth. It was so real that I could relate to the same pain I was experiencing in the present day moment. I levitated above my body in the meditation as the feeling of pain was unbearable, but followed through with the meditation as I felt I was there to experience this event for a reason.

I came back from the meditation feeling like I had connected with a piece of my lost soul and now had a feeling of calmness. From that day I have not once experienced the stomach condition. The stomach issue that hindered my life had been resolved by a transformational meditation with a Time Travel (Time Link) crystal — connecting with an old wound of the past. This experience has awoken my consciousness and knowledge to the Crystal Kingdom and I know that this is one of my life purposes, to pass on this incredible information to others.

Sarah Jane Starr (O'Brien), Busselton, Western Australia, Australia
Crystal Gaia — crystal awareness workshops for children and teens
crystalgaia@westnet.com.au

When my ex-husband and I separated we needed to sell our house in order for us all to move forward. It had been on the market for nine months and I was praying to spirit to please release us and sell this house as I so desperately wanted to move forward with my life. I decided to let go of the thoughts about the house not selling and to put it out to the universe. A month later we had two couples coming to view the house. I had a strong feeling to set up a crystal grid in order to help emanate the energy, but then got conflicting thoughts and had a message to put away all my crystal grids to unclutter the house and to work esoterically with crystals.

I set the intention and space by sitting in the middle of the open plan living area connected with divine light while invoking the angels and spirit guides. I visualised six large Clear Quartz points in the areas of the whole house to create a six-pointed star. I then sent loving thoughts, joy and harmony into the quartz points in the centre of my grid to build up the energy, and expanded it from my heart chakra in order to visualise activating the grid. I left the house just in time as the real estate agent had arrived with the people wanting to view the house. The next day we had a call that there was an offer made on the house. By using positive thoughts and working with the essence of crystals, we were able to sell the house and were able to all start our new journeys.

✦ ✦ ✦

Christopher Lock, Adelaide, South Australia, Australia
The Blue Merlin Healing Academy
chris@bluemerlinhealingacademy.com.au
www.bluemerlinhealingacademy.com.au

During the mid 1990s the second crystal I ever bought was a Lapis Lazuli cut in the shape of a pyramid. I used this to take a friend on a guided meditation, for a bit of fun. We lay down on our backs and put our pyramids on our foreheads covering our third eyes. My friend used a Rose Quartz pyramid.

We relaxed our breathing, and I began leading us on a journey . . . this experience was unusual in that I guided us back to one of my past lives in which I was killed with a sword. Not only did my friend see all that I was describing, but afterwards when we discussed it, she had seen images that I had seen but not described to her during the meditation. At the time this experience confirmed for me what powerful tools crystals are. It opened me up further to their energies and also proved to me that in fact we do have past lives, and crystals can assist in deep cleansing and releasing of past lives.

✦ ✦ ✦

Mandy Heritage PhD, Brisbane, Queensland, Australia
mandyheritage@yahoo.com.au

My most profound experience with a crystal was a meditation with the Divine Temple (Cathedral Lightbrary) Crystal. We went inside the crystal to connect with the Akashic Records. The place where the Akashic Records were stored was an incredible, heavenly place with thousands of temples, each one for a certain person. Inside my temple were rows and rows of books on shelves, all containing information from my lifetimes, every thought, emotion and experience. I found my book for this lifetime and when I opened it I needed to ask a question — 'What was my life purpose?' Nothing came to me for a minute or two, but then I felt it. I felt that every experience I'd ever had had prepared me to be a healer and to help people. Everything, the abuse, the anger, the alone-ness, everything. Every experience, the good, the bad, the ugly, had made me the person I am today and that makes me the perfect healer. In fact, all those experiences gave me the tools to be a healer, to have the understanding of how people felt when horrible things happened to them. It was incredible to know that. To know that every bad thing that had happened to me was meant to be and had to be for me to do the job I came to do. That experience with the Divine Temple Crystal (Cathedral Lightbrary) has changed my life; it gave my life meaning and gave me peace from the trauma that had occurred. It shone light where there was dark and for that I am forever grateful.

✦ ✦ ✦

Ann Kuzub, Gladstone, South Australia, Australia
annkuzub@bigpond.com

In 2006 I went into a crystal shop where an amazing crystal was sitting in a cabinet. I had an immediate connection to it. It was labelled as a Goddess (Isis) Crystal, which I related to as I had a desire to visit Egypt, so the Isis name was appropriate. The first time I meditated with this crystal I was drawn into the wisdom of this amazing crystal, helping with problem solving, showing the solution to health problems, giving comfort in times of sadness and stress, and sharing the ability of using it during healing sessions, even a successful outcome to a digestive problem. I used it during several healing sessions on clients, especially when they were unsure of the way to handle a situation. We would ask this amazing stone to please help with a solution during the session and it was very successful, with everyone receiving guidance and a possible way to approach the situation. I also used it during healing for blockages in the chakra system. During a wonderful crystal healing course I discovered that my Goddess (Isis) Crystal was in fact a Teacher (Master) Crystal. For over five years this beautiful crystal had been with me continuously, under my pillow, in my pocket, at courses, and it accompanied me on two visits to Egypt.

About five weeks before the crystal teachers course in Heartland in 2011, I was given a message during a healing that I had to bury this crystal. This was a bit of a rollercoaster ride as I had a very strong attachment to it, but I dug a hole and buried it under a rose bush, knowing that I could dig it up whenever I wanted. I was very tempted to dig it up to take with me to Heartland but I left it in the garden. This crystal has now become part of my healing crystals and will be a powerful Teaching (Master) Crystal for me to use in my workshops. I will continue to meditate with it and absorb the wisdom of Mother Earth, which will be renewed and reinforced.

✦ ✦ ✦

Jess Bowe, Sydney, New South Wales, Australia
We All Have Wings
jess@weallhavewings.net.au
www.weallhavewings.net.au

My journey with crystals has been one of self-realisation and understanding.

I cannot tell you when crystals came into my life as they have always been with me. However, my journey has not always been smooth sailing since crystals came into my life. I sometimes ask myself, 'When did crystals come into my life?' Was it when my godfather gifted me my first one when I was a baby, or when I began to understand and respect the amazing knowledge and power they share with us, or maybe it was when I was selected to be a representative of The Academy of Crystal Awakening and share the knowledge of the Crystal Kingdom with others. But when does a journey really begin and when does it end? In my belief we are in a constant cycle of new beginnings and new experiences.

As I cannot distinguish a time when crystals were not in my life, I will tell you about an experience that has guided me on my journey.

In 2005 my mother passed away after a long battle with emphysema. Shocked to the very core by the reality of life and death, I felt very open, exposed and alone. It was at this moment of weakness that I was touched by spirit. I could feel and see my mother's presence everywhere I went. I could no longer deny that life had meaning and my actions had purpose. For the first time in my life I consciously searched for my purpose and the role I was to play in the world. Every time I asked for a door to open it would, and waiting behind it was an amazing mentor, ready and waiting to expand my knowledge and experience.

Crystals have enabled me to understand and reflect on choices, events and circumstances that have happened in my life. Crystals have supported and loved me unconditionally, helping me to see beyond the situation, peeling away the veils of illusion that have kept me trapped in damaging patterns and assisting me to release old karma.

My journey with crystals is far from over as I endeavour to shine a light of unconditional love here on Earth, supporting others to see beyond their own limitations and assisting them to know their true potential. Sometimes it's only when we stand alone in the darkness that we are able to see the light shine down on us.

We all have wings, may we all fly together.

✦ ✦ ✦

Following is an interview I did with online magazine Spirit Voice.

Rachelle Charman is unquestionably one of the leading crystal healers in Australia. Her passion and inspiration to spread her love and knowledge of crystals to others has created one of the biggest crystal training organisations in Australia.

The global popularity of her teachings sowed the seeds for The Academy of Crystal Awakening to develop, creating a ripple effect of crystal healers across Australia, New Zealand and beyond.

Rachelle's teachings come from her deep-rooted connection to Mother Earth and have been inspired by her mentors. Reconnecting with her instinctive knowledge of crystals and natural healing techniques has allowed Rachelle to transform her students' own intuitive healing abilities with incredible results.

A remarkable and authentic woman creating a new level of healing straight from the heart and Mother Earth.

Rachelle, we really must start by discussing what led you down this path of healing. Do you remember your first crystal experience?

The first time I had an experience with the Crystal Kingdom truly changed me forever. It was one of the most powerful and insightful experiences of my life. I will try and share with you a short version of my experience with you so you can get an idea of the power of the Crystal Kingdom and its healing.

The first half of my life I was quite lost and running from a deep pain deep inside. I experienced a lot of sadness, depression and anxiety and most of the time life was a struggle just to get out of bed in the mornings. Throughout this part of my life I searched for many ways to hide from the pain, and found myself in unhealthy relationships and eventually into drugs to hide the pain.

My crystal awakening happened in the year 2000 when I believe there was a shift in the energy on the planet to support many people through a transition. I had been gifted an Amethyst Crystal and had purchased a Quartz Crystal the week before. This night I was sitting on the couch with both crystals in my hands, going into what I know now to be a trance. Suddenly my whole body started to vibrate and at first was quite scary, as I had no idea what was happening. For three days and three nights I did not eat and was in this potent spiritual awakening sparked by the Crystal Kingdom. It brought love and light into every single cell of my being, into the dark places inside that I had been running from. It eased the pain and filled me with love and compassion, feelings that I had not felt in my life so far. I remembered experiences from the past would arise in my mind, and while being in this sacred space of spiritual and profound awareness I could see why these traumas had happened in my life, and for the first time was able to see the gifts in such pain.

This awakening set me free from my old chains and restraints that I had put upon myself and invited me to look at life in a new way. For the first time I felt love for myself and a deep sense of inner peace of my soul. The fog had lifted from my heart and my soul, and I started to see the light at the end of the tunnel. I started to feel hope for my future and inspiration for what was to come. Many people call this the dark night of the soul and I like to call it the awakening of the soul. From this experience it started me on my spiritual path and sparked a deep passion inside to understand more about crystals and healing. I also wanted to share this awakening with others who also feel lost in their life, hoping to give some sort of inspiration and hope.

I completed three intense crystal healing workshops with a beautiful lady, my teacher Maggie Vrinda Ross. Everything we learnt, I experienced

— it was like a flower blossoming within as I started to remember the sacred healing power of crystals. I believe if you are attracted to crystals you have known them before, so it becomes a process of remembering and reawakening this sacred knowledge within.

This was over 11 years ago and I now have a crystal academy with over 3000 students and 28 teachers sharing the love and wisdom of the Crystal Kingdom around the world, living my dream and passion.

You developed The Academy of Crystal Awakening to share your knowledge, so others could benefit and use crystals to heal. Have you found your students find their own inner transformations and healing throughout the learning process? I mean, most people would first think of learning to heal others without even considering the effect on themselves.

Yes it is amazing witnessing the deep healing that occurs in the workshops when you support people to be their own master and follow their own guidance and intuition. The students receive a deep sense of self and empowerment, being encouraged to have their own experience and bring through their own wisdom. This is how I learnt what I know from the Crystal Kingdom and know in my heart that others too receive and learn this way. My intention for all the students is that they spark their own wisdom and knowledge, and this is validated in the workshop, and powerful healing can occur on many levels, especially a deep honouring and believing in yourself. I also believe that when you facilitate other people's healing you are also healing yourself, they go hand in hand.

What do you think makes your techniques and teachings on crystals so different to other workshops currently available?

The difference in my crystal healing processes is that we work very closely with the Earth and the teachings are very grounded and tangible.

Most of the teachings invite us to look inside of ourselves instead of giving our power away to outside influences. The crystals teach us to open our hearts and love ourselves for who we are right here and now. As I mentioned before, my teachings highlight that everyone has their own wisdom and knowledge.

> You spent some time among Peruvian shamans and native healers in the Amazons, which must have been an incredible, enriching experience. How did this adventure come to be and what sort of things did you learn whilst there?

Wow, that's a big question and I could spend a lifetime sharing this answer; however, I will save it for my next book and I will keep it short and sweet for now.

I had been called to travel to Peru ever since I was young. I knew that I would travel there one day and there would be someone special to meet me there. I was blessed enough to travel to Peru and around the world in 2005. It was once again another truly amazing and life changing experience. It was like walking in to the book, the Celestine Prophecy, when I arrived in Peru. I knew in my heart that I was going to meet a very special person that would have a huge impact on my life, I knew this to be true deep in my bones.

I was sitting in my hotel lobby in Cusco one day knowing this meeting was close and even writing this in my diary and this group of people entered into the room. The energy of these people took my attention and I sat watching what they were doing. They all seemed very happy and they were in some sort of powerful energy. After a while two men came over to me; one could speak a little English and the other could only speak Spanish and the local native tongue. They both looked at me and one man whispered something to the other. This man then said to me in broken English, 'You are the angel you have been looking for'. Of all the things someone could say to me at the time those words were perfect as I had just finished working for Doreen Virtue, the angel lady, and have a deep connection to the Angelic Realm. Tears started flowing down my face and my heart opened with the knowing that I was in the right place at the right time. Then both men sat down with me and I meet my shaman, Edwin. He could not speak English and I could not speak his language so the other gentleman, by the name of Jesus, was our interpreter. Edwin shared with me that he knew I was arriving and he invited me to travel around Peru with him to many sacred sights, doing many sacred initiations and ceremonies. This was the awakening of my shamanic wisdom and understanding of the healing ways of our ancient land.

Edwin would come and pick me up from the hotel and we would travel for hours in the car in silence; however, it showed me that the connection of the heart goes beyond words. I remember vividly this day when he took me up into the mountains and placed me into this cave, picked up a stone, put it in my hand, then put my hand on my heart. He closed my eyes and left the cave. I sat down and was there for what seemed like hours. After a while I started getting a little concerned that he had not returned and opened my eyes. Edwin was nowhere to be seen. I started going into a panic, thinking I had been left on a mountain in Peru and no-one knew where I was. Many fears of abandonment started to arise in me; however, something amazing was happening. I could feel the love and support of the cave of the earth, it was amazing. Then Edwin showed up with a grin on his face, like he knew what was happening. He then took me to the river and did the same thing.

At the time I really did not understand in depth what was happening and it took many years to integrate; however, I understand now he was introducing me the elements. I had many incredible experiences with Edwin and the land in Peru; however, the most amazing part of this for me was once again all these experiences sparked an awakening or knowing deep within me of this ancient wisdom of healing and the Earth. It was not outside of me, something I had to learn or search for, it was deep in my spirit, a remembering of this powerful wisdom within.

I also believe that we all have this innate intelligence to tap into and tune into this ancient wisdom of the land, and connect to and work with the laws of nature. You don't have to sit on the mountain with a shaman to receive the healing love and blessing of the Mother Earth. Once again it is our birthright here on Earth. As long as you are born into this wonderful Earth you have this knowledge in your blood and bones, and the ability to tap into this medicine and healing energy of the Earth. Spending time in Peru and in the jungle of South America changed my life in so many ways, but ultimately it brought me closer to myself and our Divine Mother Earth. It's funny how we travel all around the world looking for answers to realise they were inside all along.

> You have many levels to your trainings which would contain many processes and understandings about healing with crystal. Can you suggest an all-purpose crystal for healing and maybe share a quick technique for our readers to try themselves?

Oh there are so many crystals that I would love to share with you, let me introduce to you the first crystal I ever had an experience with and that is Amethyst. This is an overall healing crystal that works on many levels. Amethyst is abundant on the Earth and very easy to get your hands on from all the gem and spiritual shops. Amethyst balances the left and right hemispheres of the brain, allowing the mind to relax and the heart to open. It is great in this day and age where we find our monkey minds racing and our busy schedules. It helps us to relax and unwind. It is also a great friend in assisting us in awakening our physic abilities and deepen our intuition. Also a great crystal to help us sleep at night.

There are various processes you can do with crystals; however, I would like to share a very simple yet powerful one with you. Simply sit in a peaceful environment (preferably in nature) with your cleansed crystal. Take a few deep, calming breaths. Place your crystal on your heart as you breathe in this loving, supportive energy and vibration.

Then allow yourself to feel the crystal sending you its blessing and medicine. Feel it pulsating into your heart and from your heart allow this crystal energy to move into every single cell of your being. Continue breathing the crystal energy into your heart for a few minutes, then sit in silence with the crystal, absorbing its healing vibration. This is a very quick and simple way to start creating a connection to the Crystal Kingdom. Enjoy.

Is there a common misconception in regards to crystals or healing with crystals?

The only misconception I have really come across is the belief that you need qualifications to have an experience or connection. As I mentioned before it is our birthright to connect to and receive healing and support from crystals, and this happens very organically and is different for everyone.

You now have a group of highly trained teachers around Australia, who are then training practitioners. Did you ever think your academy would expand so quickly? It is truly inspirational seeing how far one person's own spiritual journey can influence so many others. You have done an amazing job spreading your love.

Thank you, it has been such an amazing journey and ride creating the Academy and it has grown fast very quickly. I first had the vision and awareness of creating the Academy when I arrived home from my year's travels around the world. I was working for an amazing man by the name of John Demartini who asked me a very powerful question — 'Why are you here Rachelle and what do you love to do?' This was the first time anyone had ever really asked me this question and the first time I had ever posted it to myself. He shared with me that we are all sparks of the divine and are here on Earth to share this love, and what better way to do it than create your work around what you love. This resonated very deeply with me and as soon as I asked myself what is was that I loved the visions and answers came very strong and quick. I realised I wanted to have an academy and share my love and passion about crystals and healing and travel the world. The only thing that seemed to be in my way was the fear of talking in front of people. I remember working with Doreen Virtue many years ago and she asked me to come on stage with 1000 people to share with them how to cleanse their crystals. I did not know she was going to do this and it felt like the death walk from the side of the stage. I will never forget this defining moment in my life as I looked at the crowd and the first thing that came out of my month was 'Now everyone close your eyes'. Everyone closed their eyes and I realised that no-one could see me anymore and, gee, did I thank the angels for that one. It was a funny yet powerful moment in my life where I took everyone through a meditation to cleanse their crystals.

After the meditation two women came up to me and showed me their crystals that had broken through the process. I realised then that this was powerful and if I could stand up in front of 1000 people and not die I could teach a class of 20 to 40 people. I went on to create the Academy and have taught in front of thousands of people. Sometimes we have to feel the fear and do it anyway. Don't wait for the fear to go away as you will be waiting forever as the fear is created when you don't step into your power and walk your dreams. I have come to realise that sometimes our dreams and visions are coated with fear; however, when we find the courage and strength to face that fear we are also blessed with the gifts of our essences and spirit that is our truth. Along the way I have had many self-doubts in my life and myself; however, I feel if you do what you love and love what you do, manifestation is organic and you will live your dreams and shine your light no matter what.

For someone looking at doing a Crystal Awakening workshop, what experience do they need and how do your workshop levels work?

Our workshops are created for people from all walks of life with no previous healing practices to people who have been on their healing journey for years. In the Academy we have three levels of crystal healing workshops that are accredited by the National Federation of Healers in Brisbane. We have the foundation and intermediate workshops that are run purely by the accredited teachers of the Academy. I have personally created all the workshops from my own experiences and wisdom handed down from my teachers. The workshops are for anyone looking to love and know more of themselves, the Crystal Kingdom and Mother Earth. I no longer teach the foundation and intermediate here in Australia; however, am taking it all around the world. In Australia I personally run the advanced level which is based around many powerful processes, unleashing your shamanic healing powers and working with many different medicines of the Earth. I also run a one-day basic workshop on shamanism and crystals and it is a great way to start to tap into your own innate healing abilities, working with the laws and love of nature.

Do you do one-on-one healing sessions or predominantly spend your time teaching?

I love to do one-on-one healing and have not had much time over the last few years to be able to do it all. It is very exciting that recently I have been called by spirit and the Crystal Kingdom to do more one-on-one sessions with people and I am loving it. I truly feel blessed, and what an honour to guide and support another soul on this planet to love more of themselves, and to share in such a sacred experience to dance with the healing energy and love of the universe.

Source: www.spiritsvoice.net/RachelleCharman

INDEX

higher ctd
    self 22, 36, 57, 72, 79, 89, 140, 144,
        145, 184, 197, 210
Himalayas 177
homeopathic 28
honesty 72, 223
hope 72, 109
hospitalisation 72
human psyche 114
humanity 153
humility 221

'I am' presence 36, 197
ideas 69, 74, 124, 156, 174, 181
illusion 86, 88
imagination 55, 56, 72, 124, 210
immune system 54, 72
impotency 72
independent 127
infection 72
infinite 163, 225
initiation 123, 166, 184
injury 109
inner
    chambers 175
    child 59, 72, 93, 94, 115, 142
    conflict 134
    darkness 131
    peace 54, 72, 87, 121, 125, 140, 193,
        196, 218
    realms 120, 143, 186
innocence 59, 205
insect bites 72
insensitivity 54, 115
insight 35, 56, 72, 90, 110, 116,122, 149,
    163, 187
insomnia 72
inspiration 61, 72, 93, 124, 148, 156, 174,
    203, 220, 224
instinct 33
integrate 112, 144, 163, 170, 176
intelligence 51, 60, 73, 85, 106
intention 181, 190
intimacy 34, 73, 117, 141, 145, 174
intuition 35, 56, 73, 107, 116, 121, 187,
    189, 204, 218
irrational fears 188
itching 73

Jade 35, 63, 67, 72, 74, 158
Jasper — Mookite 33, 34, 53, 67, 71, 72,
    73, 159
Jasper — Ocean 33, 67, 75, 160
Jasper — Red 33, 50, 51, 67, 68, 70,
    74, 161
jealousy 54, 73
Jet 33, 61, 72, 162
joints 73
joy 22, 34, 54, 57, 59, 60, 62, 63, 73, 93,
    94, 115, 135, 136, 180, 205, 219,
    221, 224

karmic
    contracts 112
    patterns 33, 50, 64, 73, 166
key
    to heaven 185
kidneys 73
knees 50
Kundalini 61, 73, 137, 150, 162, 199
Kunzite 34, 54, 55, 62, 67, 69, 70, 71, 72,
    73, 75, 76, 163
Kyanite — Blue 35, 55, 56, 71, 73, 74, 76,
    77, 164, 165

Labradorite 35, 62, 71, 72, 75, 165
Lapis Lazuli 11, 35, 36, 57, 64, 67, 68, 69,
    71, 72, 73, 74, 75, 77, 166
large intestine 50, 51
Larimar 35, 61, 67, 68, 70, 71, 76, 167
laughter 34, 94
leadership 73, 209
learning 73, 149, 198
legs 50, 73
Lepidolite 35, 76, 77, 168
lethargy 50, 73
letting go 56, 63, 64, 73, 90, 112, 116, 127,
    133, 145, 154, 161, 164, 168, 191
Libyan Gold Tektite 36, 73, 74, 77,
    169, 229
life
    force 61, 137, 194, 199
    mission 198, 207
    path 61,103, 207
    purpose 60, 61, 73, 103
lifting the veils 90
limitations 203
listening 55